WATERHUMMINGBIRDHOUSE
A XIKANO COLORING BOOK
BY
ISRAEL F. HAROS LOPEZ

I0494113

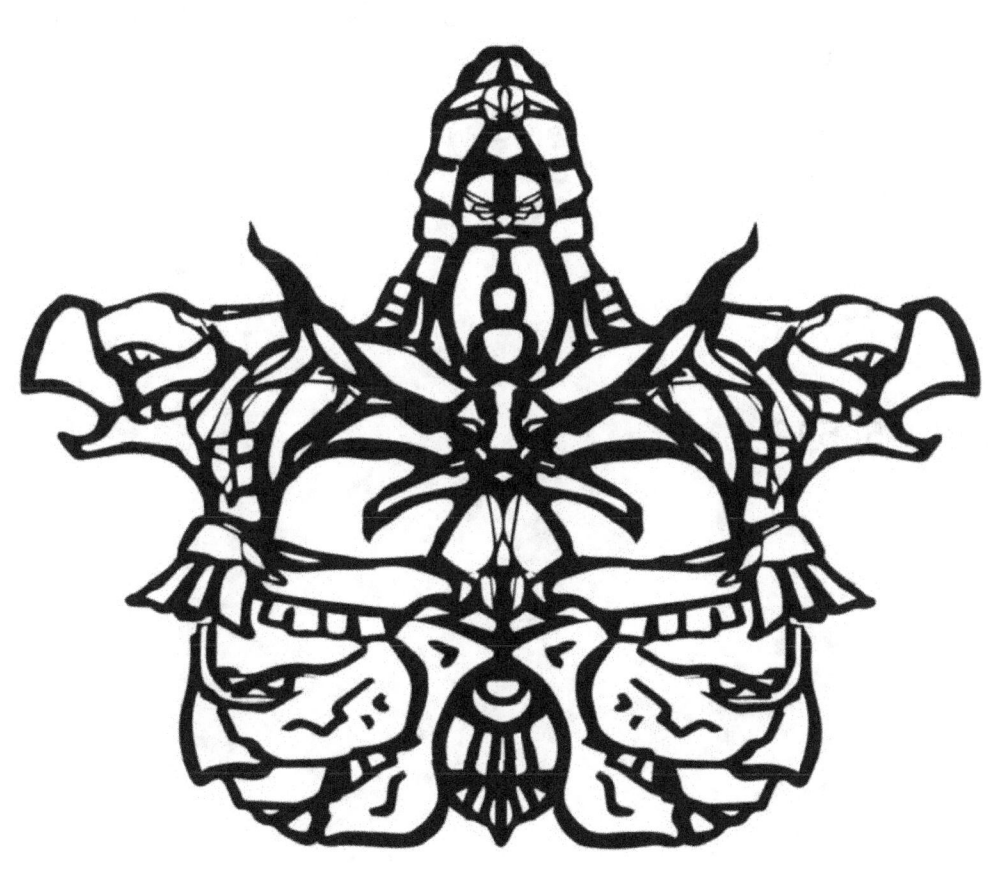

Waterhummingbirdhouse: A Xikano Coloring Book
Drawn by Israel F. Haros Lopez
Cover Design by
Israel F. Haros Lopez
Waterhummingbirdhouse : A Xikano Coloring Book.

Contact author at waterhummingbirdhouse@gmail.com
SECOND Edition Published by WATERHUMMINGBIRDHOUSE PRESS 2014

ISBN-13:
978-1499154542

ISBN-10:1499154542

Xicano Estilo Dedications,

Este libro esta dedicado a Kelatztli a.k.a Quil-a-botz-BEE, first and foremost, because you were the first one to call me uncle and change my life in that way. To Mr. Maaso and Ms. Tonanxochitl and their brillante soulzzz. Kisho and Salamon the hero twins. Metztli and Kaia who keep everybody in check. This is for Andrea la abuelita y Michelle. Tambien para Copali, Johana, Teo y Sofie the seeders of the song. Jangus for being Jangus! To Ronin and his ingenious space brothers. Eli, Gabriel and Loquito, y Benja for all being loquitos. Justin for being so much like an arrow of the sun. Roman for being his gladiator self. To Mia for the mirror you hold up with your smile. Yolimoli Yollotzin 'cuz you crazy and sooo funny!! Riley for all the courage you take to be yourself amongst us confused adults. Isae, Ethan, Junior, Josue, Cesar, Adan, Nayeli, Delilahand Zoriah my precious soulmates. To Jaime Luis for being you and your sarcastic self. ToDaniel for all your tremendous fire and for giving me the courage when I was doubting myself, walking in the garage at the right time and saying that my 9 by 12 foot housepaint abstract paintings were "REALLY NICE ISRAEL, THEY'RE REALLY NICE! I LIKE THEM ALOT ISRAEL! THEY REALLY NICE!!" To Mountain for the mountain you are already. To some newly added superheroes in my life Anajmora Ishi Sato McLaughlin and Tadhg Iolar Sato McLaughlin just for being you and teaching me so much every single time. To Santiago Olin, Amaru Agape and Quetzali Yareli for being freedom fighters since before you came out the womb. Olin don't forget to keep "dreaming outside the sun" like your papi said and practice A LOT A LOT A LOT! And you will make waaaaaay better drawing than I do! Tayeli, Amber y Maia for the water and fire you already hold. Uma and the rest of your colorado gang for all the ways color and sing this earth to life. Wesley for all ways you remind me of how to walk this earth. To Little George for smacking my drum stick when he was like 3 years old and i was 23 years old and letting me know that if i was going to drum i better pay attention, Enrique for your precious sensitive soul and lil' Jessie for your amazing smile, eyes, laughter and presence letting everybody see your SHINE!!

A los chiquiticos en Colombia tambien este libro esta dedicado a ustedes! Gracias a Isabella, Sabina, Celeste, Kusi, Taki, Kiyai, Nawel, Martin, Pepe, Suyai, Aurora, Miguel, Valentin, Valeria, Lorenzo, y Silvana por ser tan preciosos, chistosos y por toda su ayuda para la madre tierra.

To all the youth that tutored and mentored me when they thought I was mentoring or tutoring them. Somehow I got paid for the knowledge you gave me, I owe you.To the tip of the arrow known as Blanca Ortiz and all the change she is and will be for all of us. And the super she-roes known as Yovana and Alejandra who take the lead and will continue to lead. And to all those little one AND NOT SO LITTLE ONES I forgot to mention, you are embedded in my soul and I thank you for the work you came to do.Tlazocamati Cesar Teolol Cruz for self publishing, not waiting around to be accepted, and being an example in so many ways.

To Isabel and all the future little Izzies, we love you.
For all the madres and padres of these warriors. All the aunties and uncles who keep themselves in check so these young ones can flourish. To all my aunties and uncles. Para mi madre y padreen todos sentidos. To all the grandpas, grandmas, cousins, Fire,Wind, Tonantzin, Tonatiuh, Atland EVERYTHING in between. Tlazocamati.

Tlazocamati for all them "young elders" who bring their wisdom from the stars,
Izzy

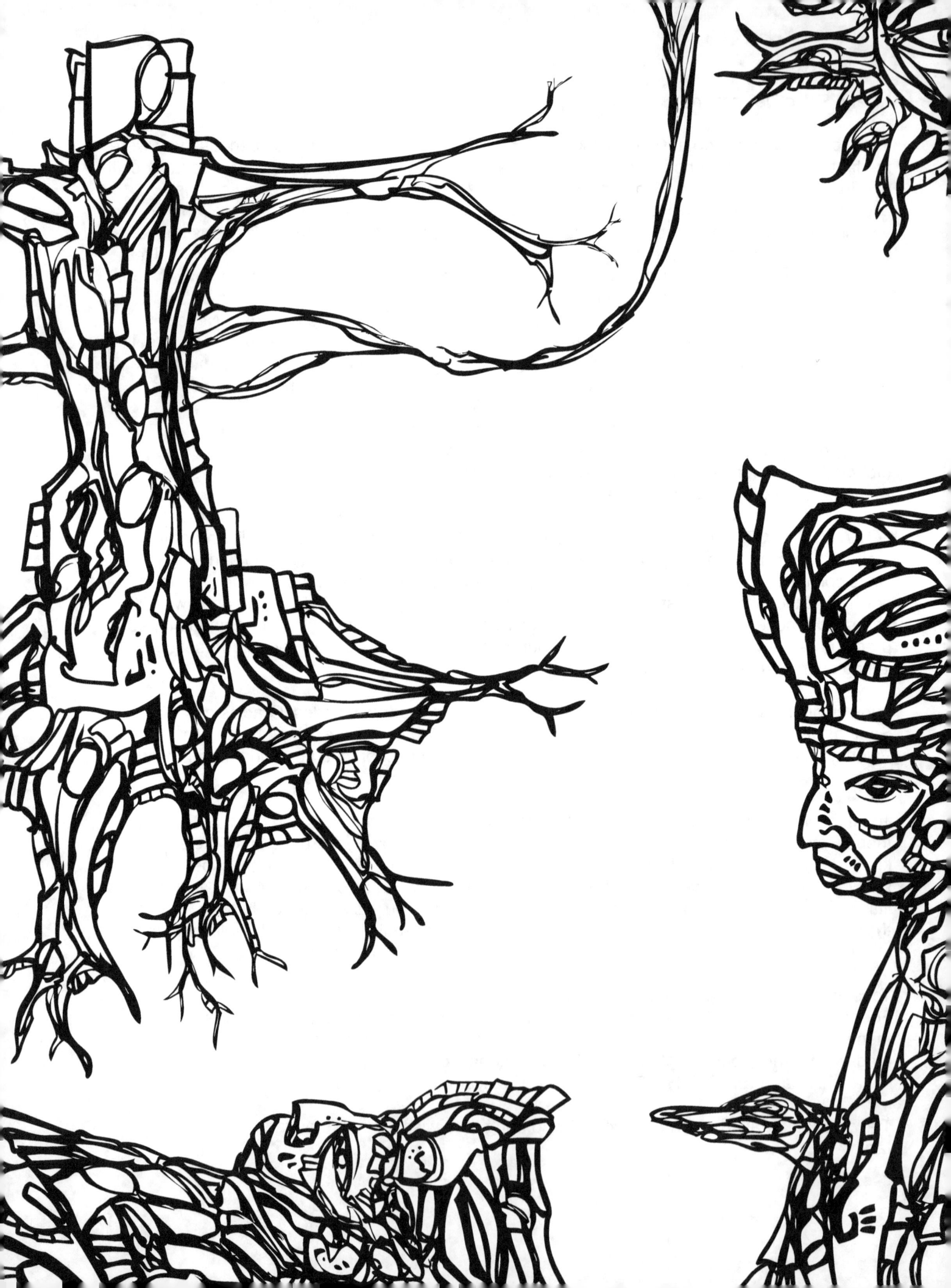

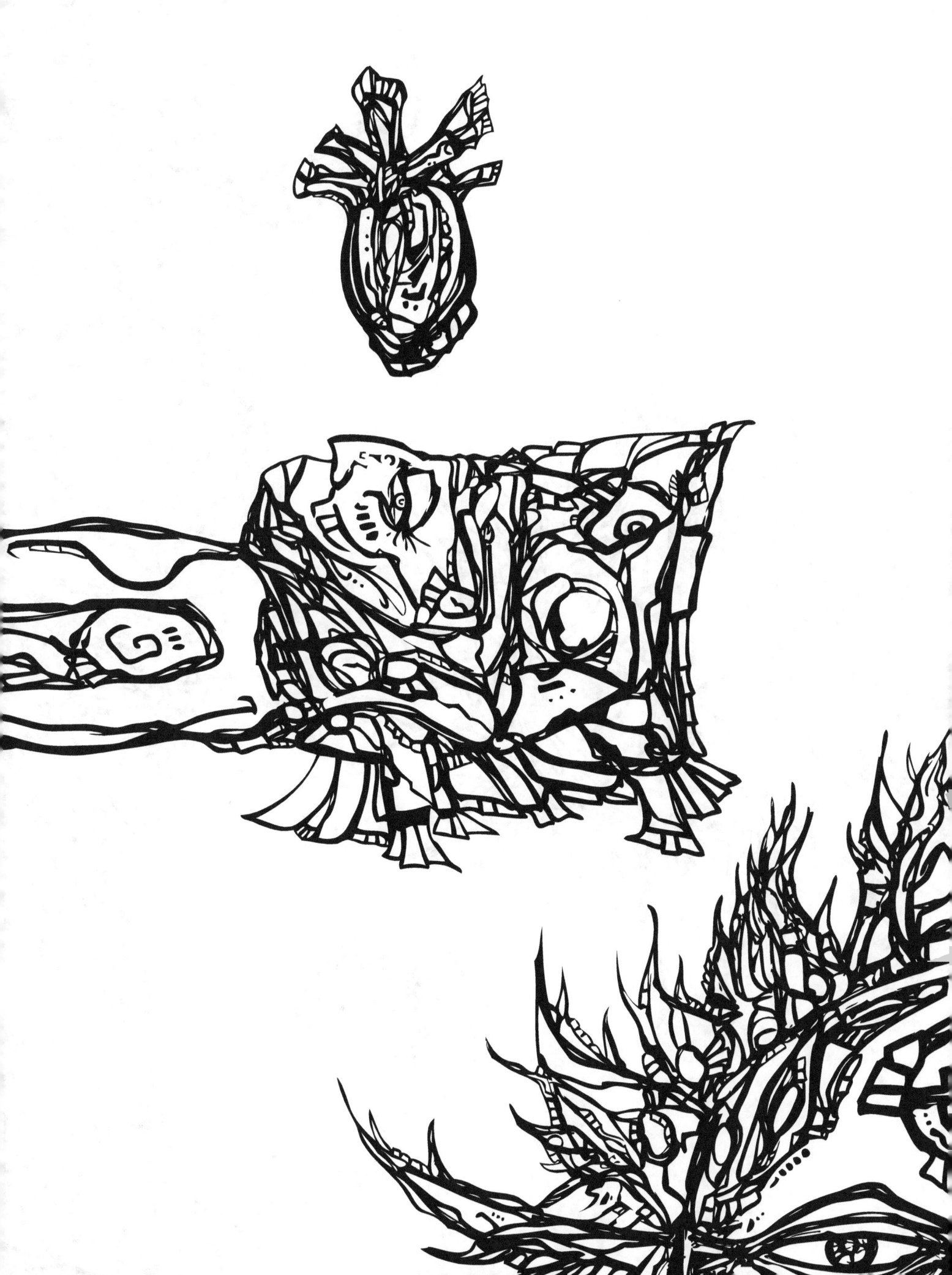

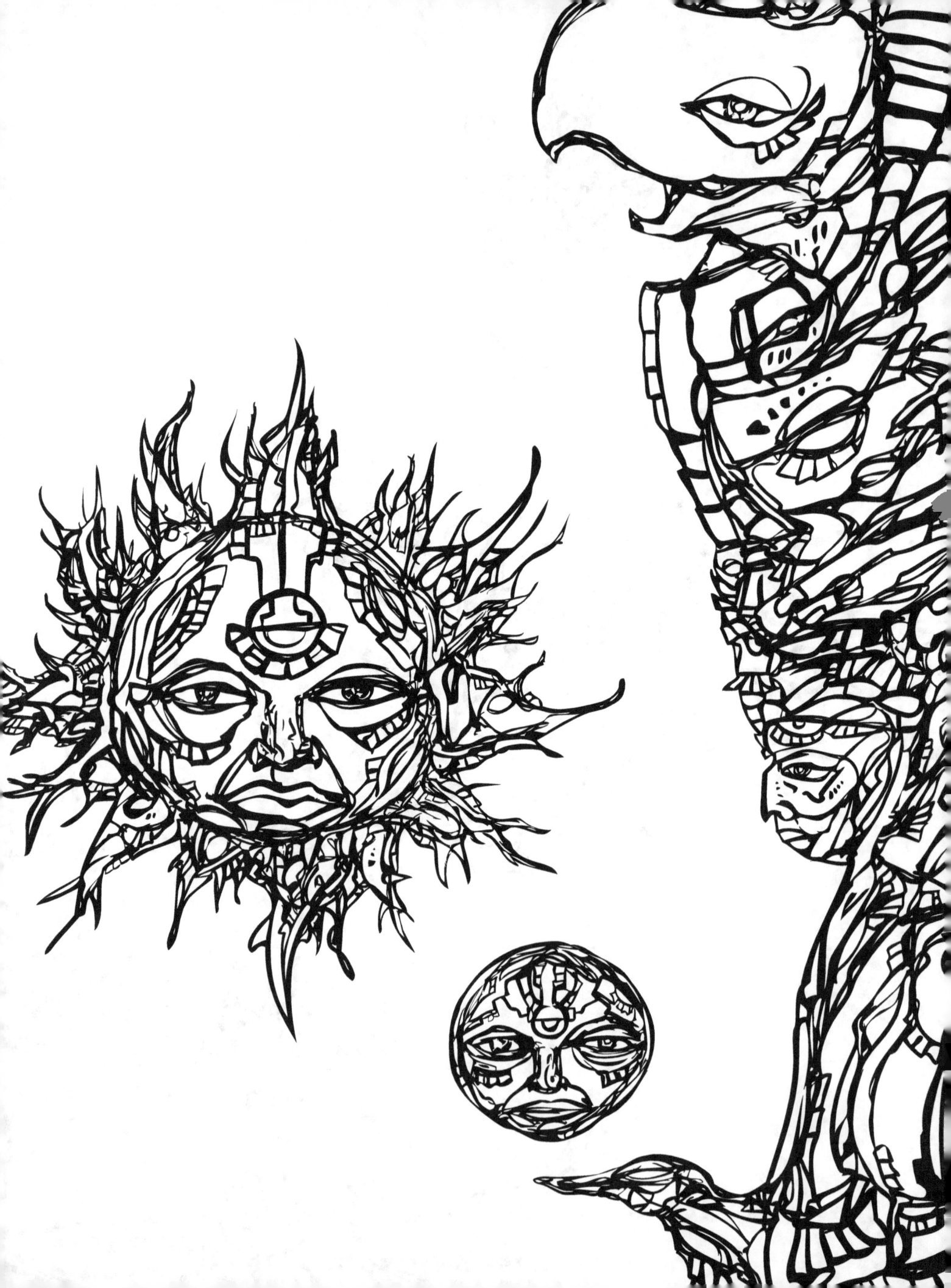

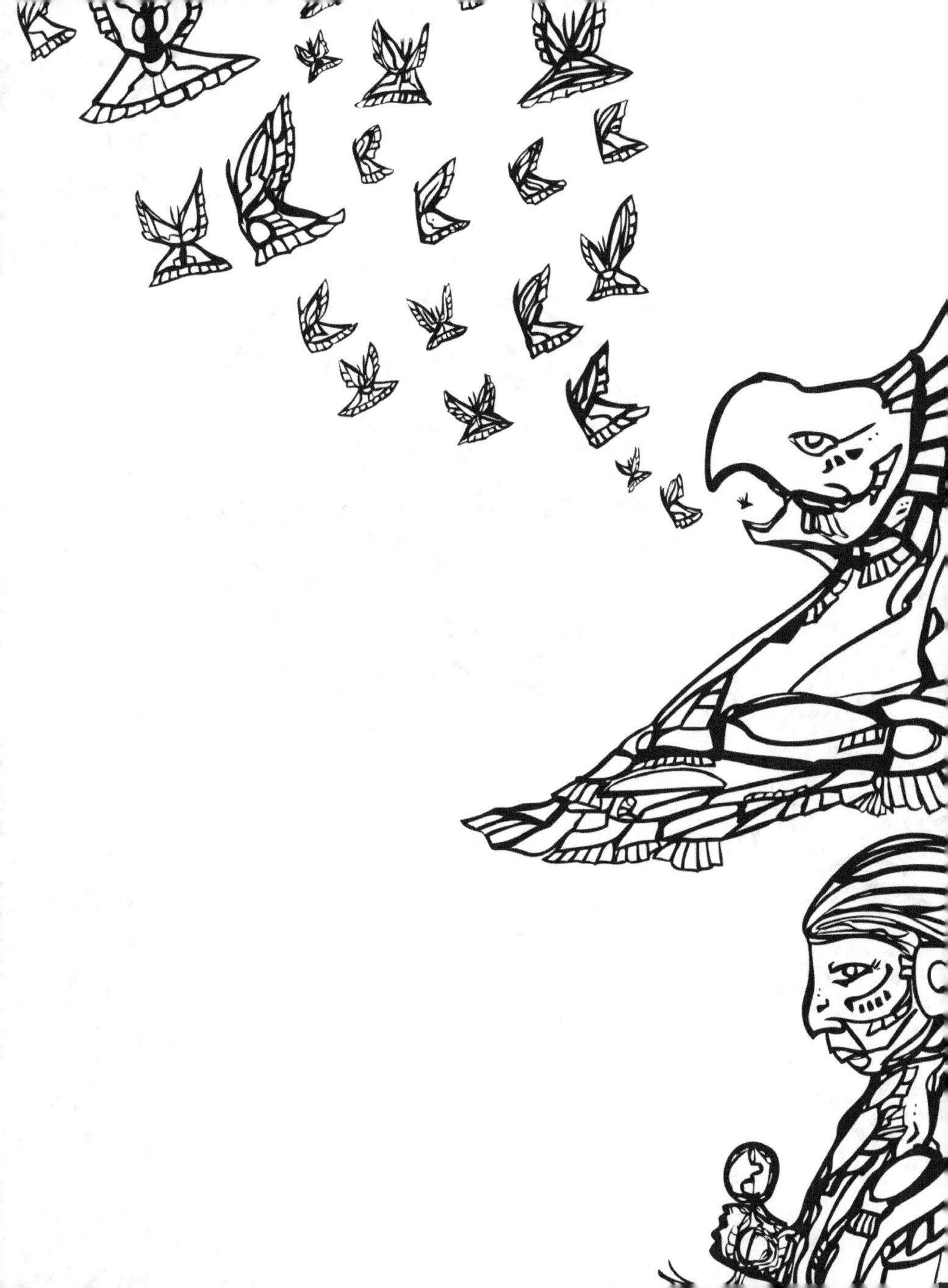

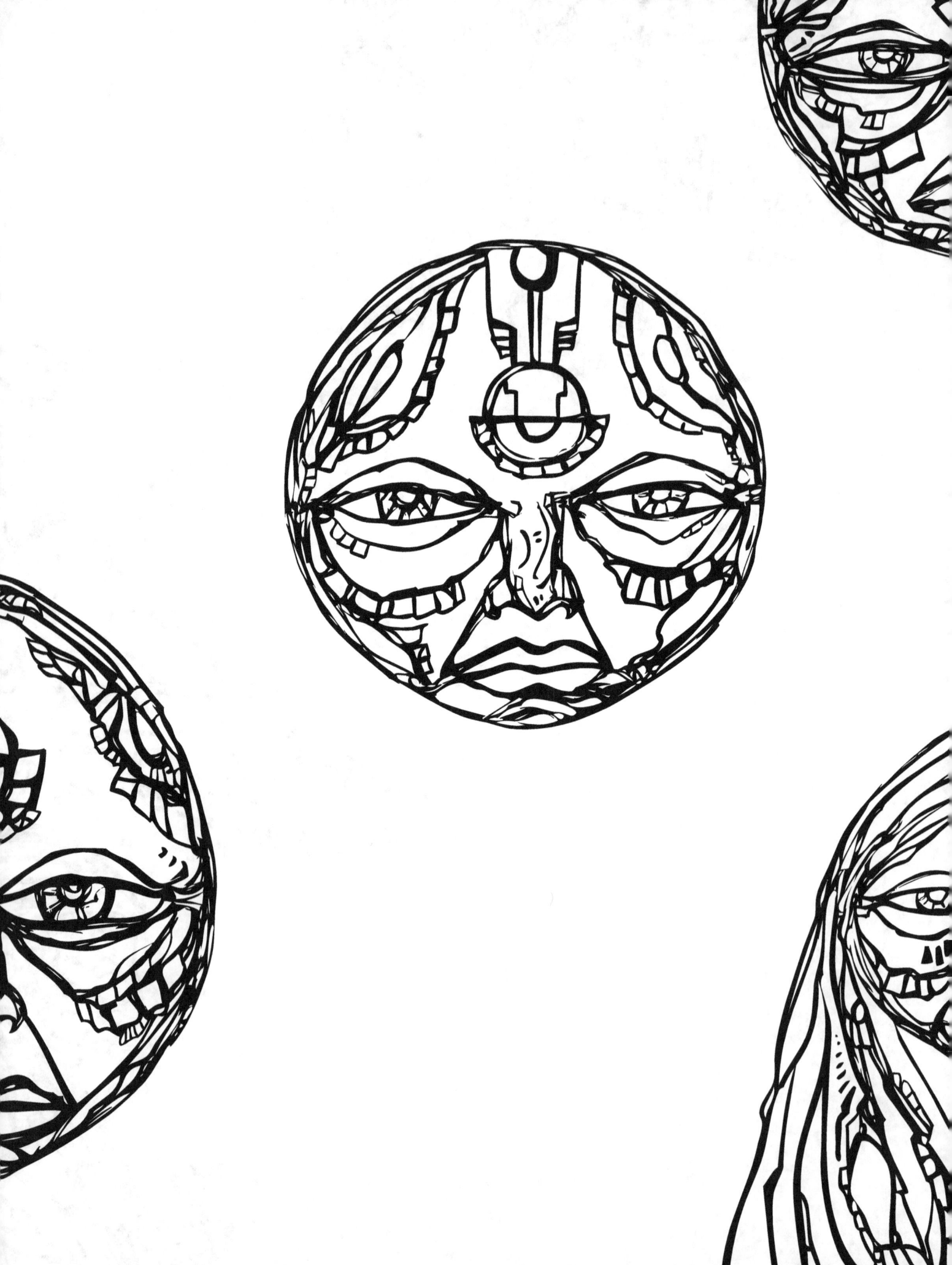

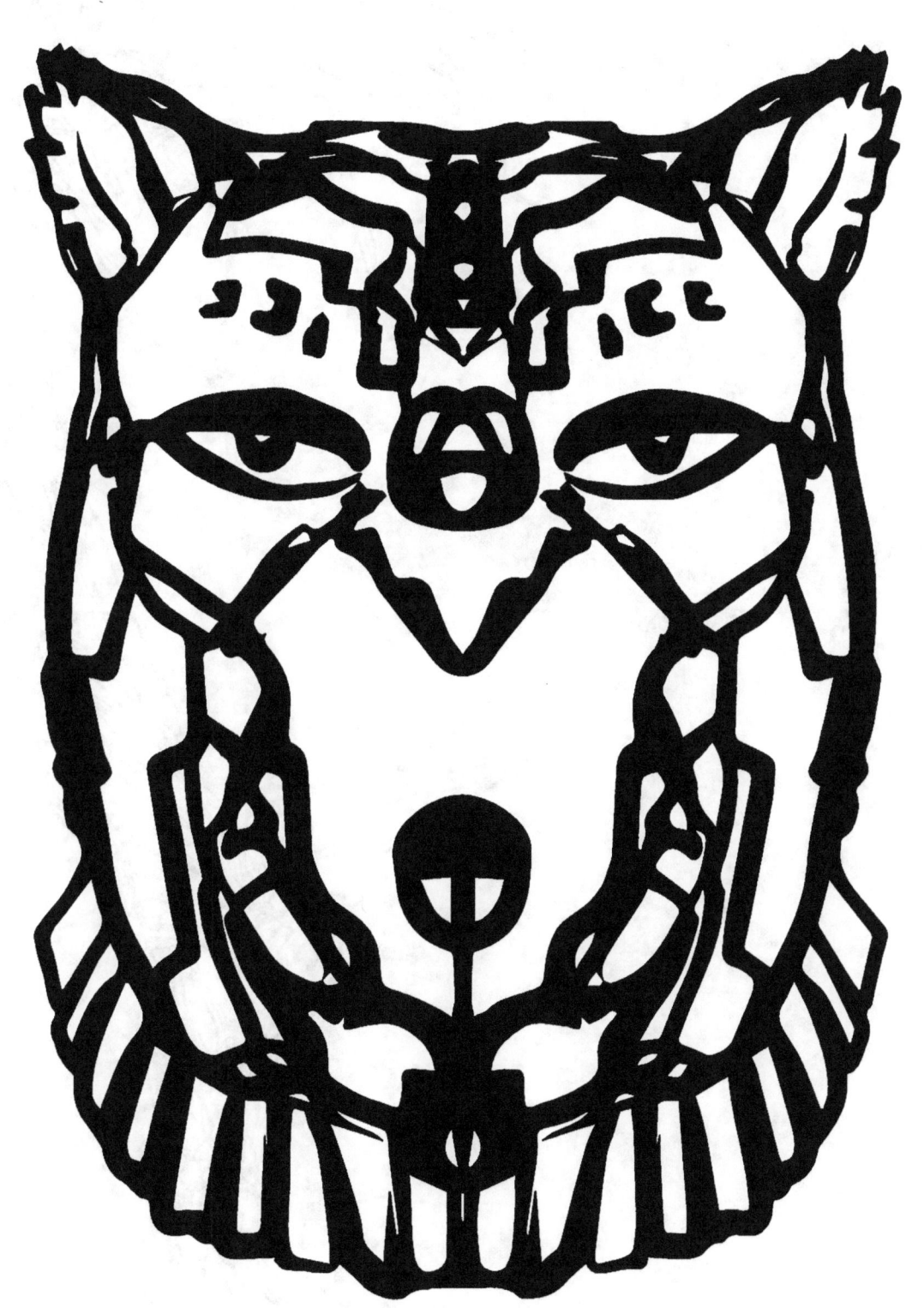

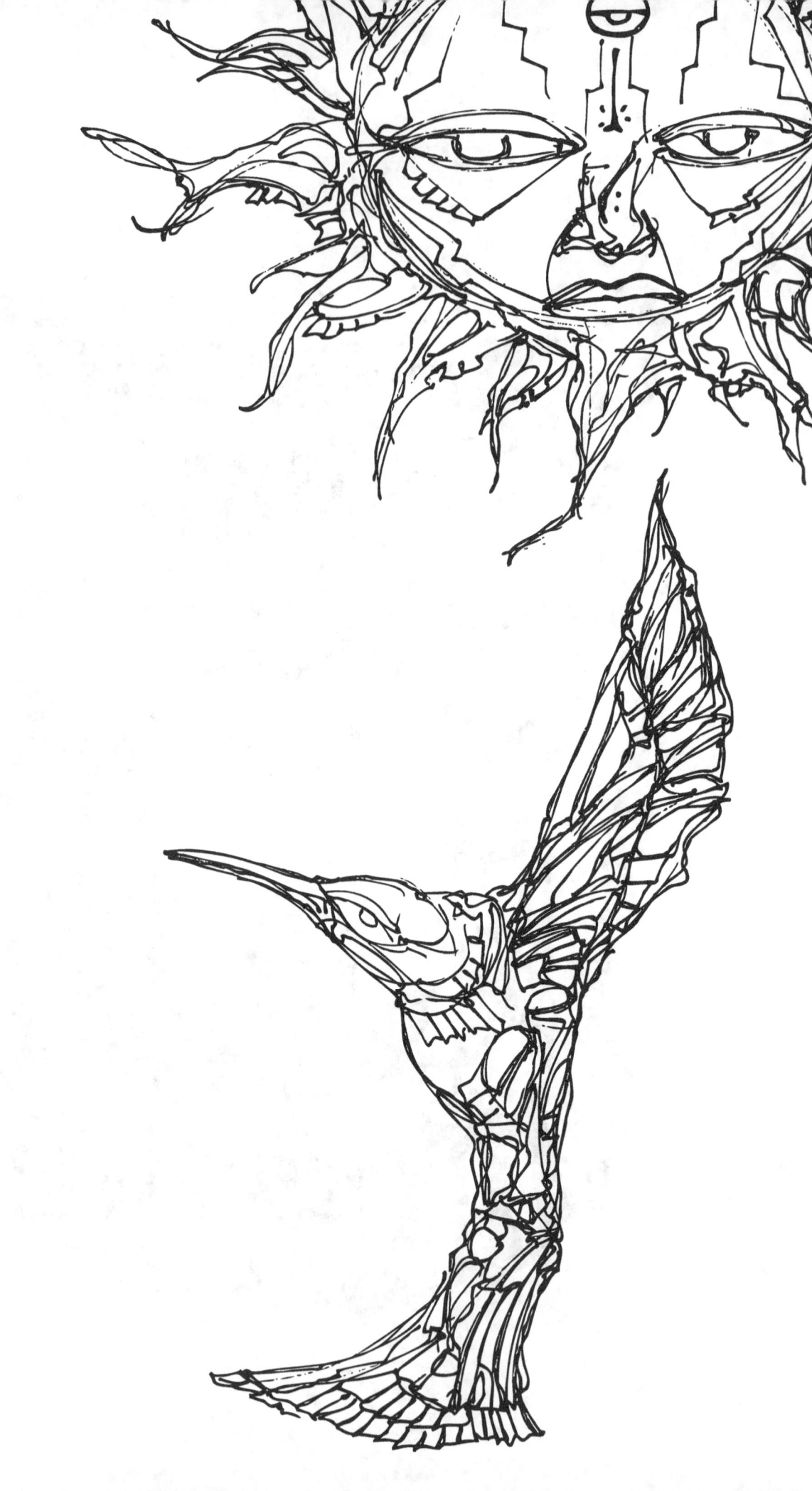

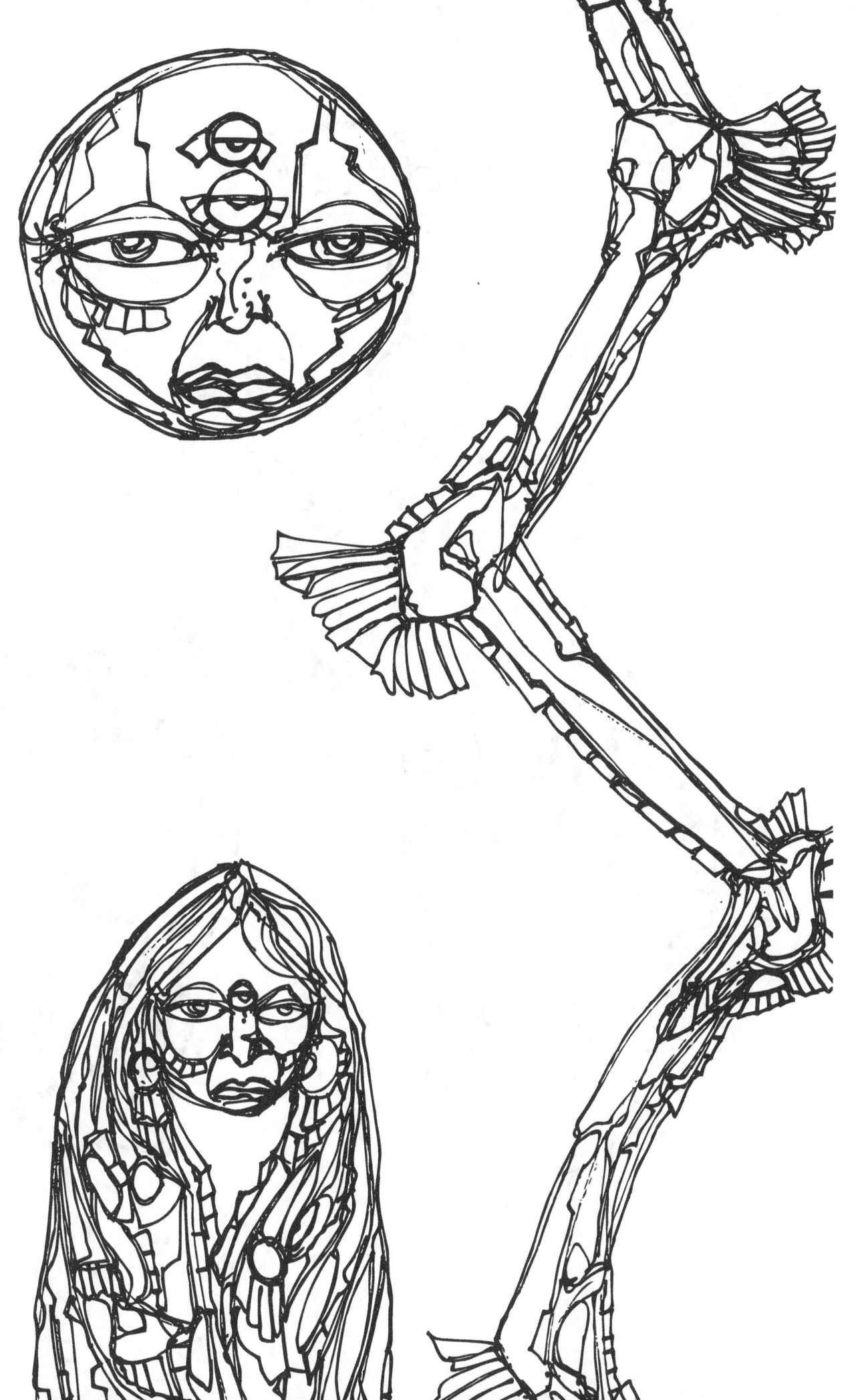

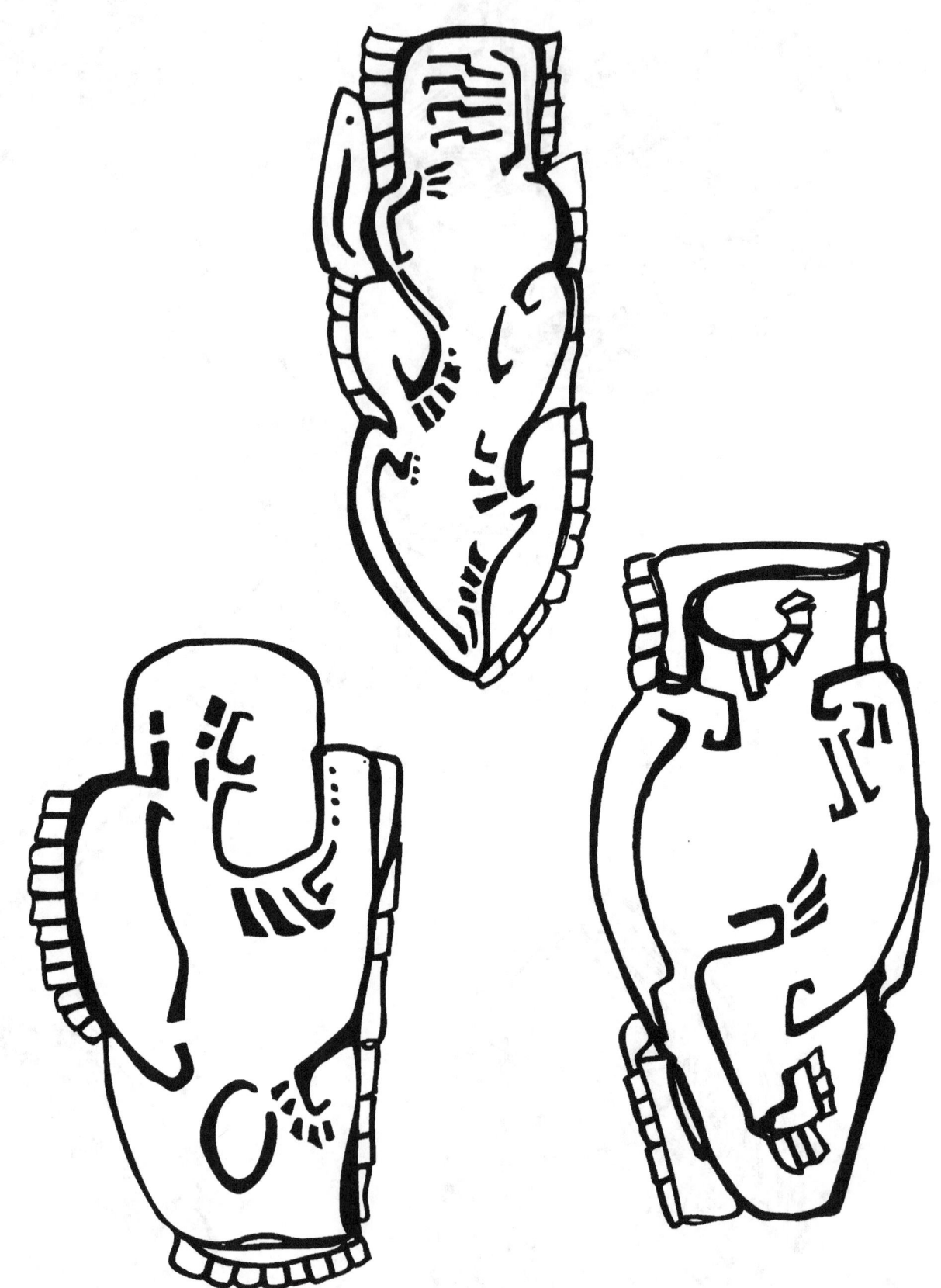

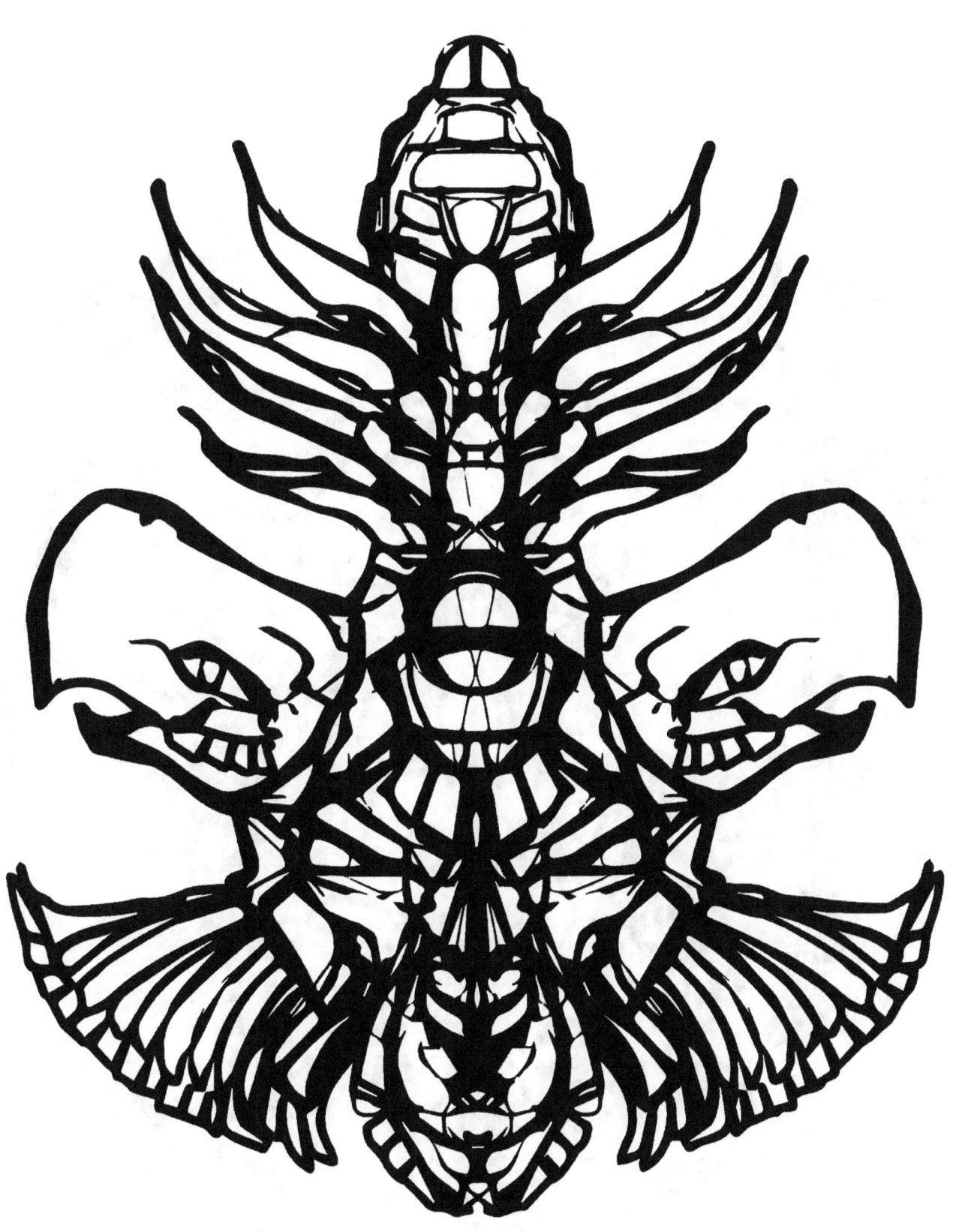

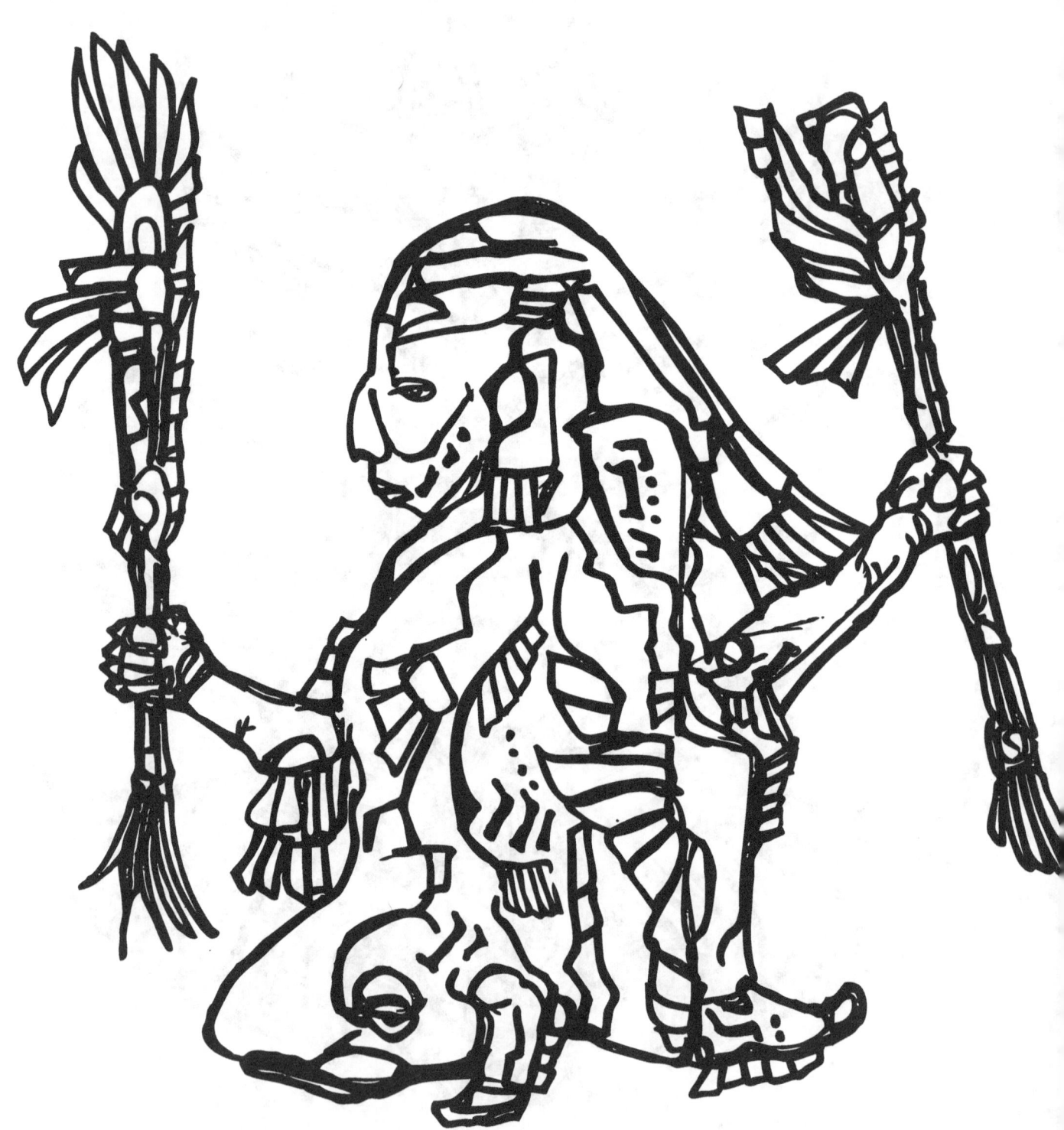

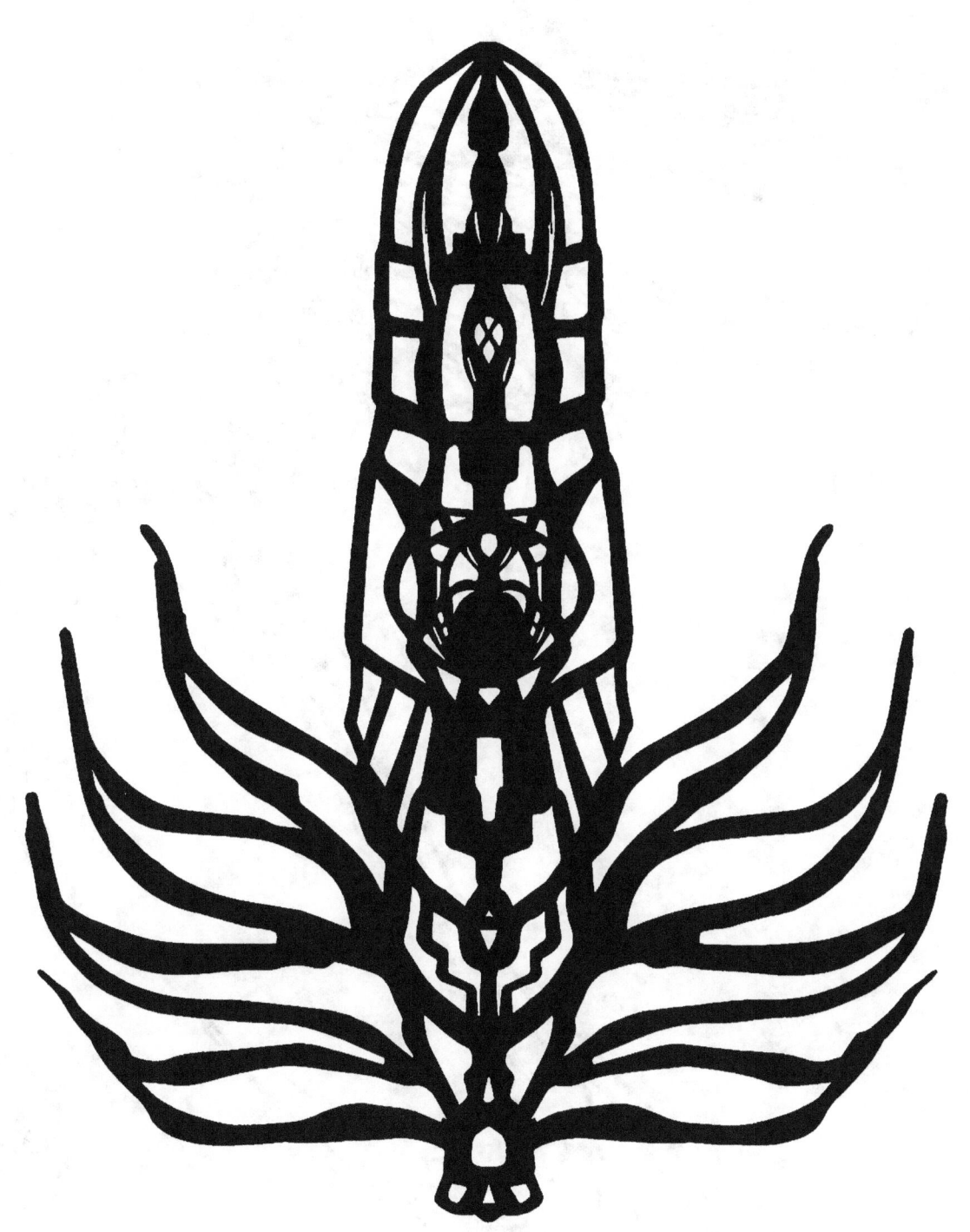

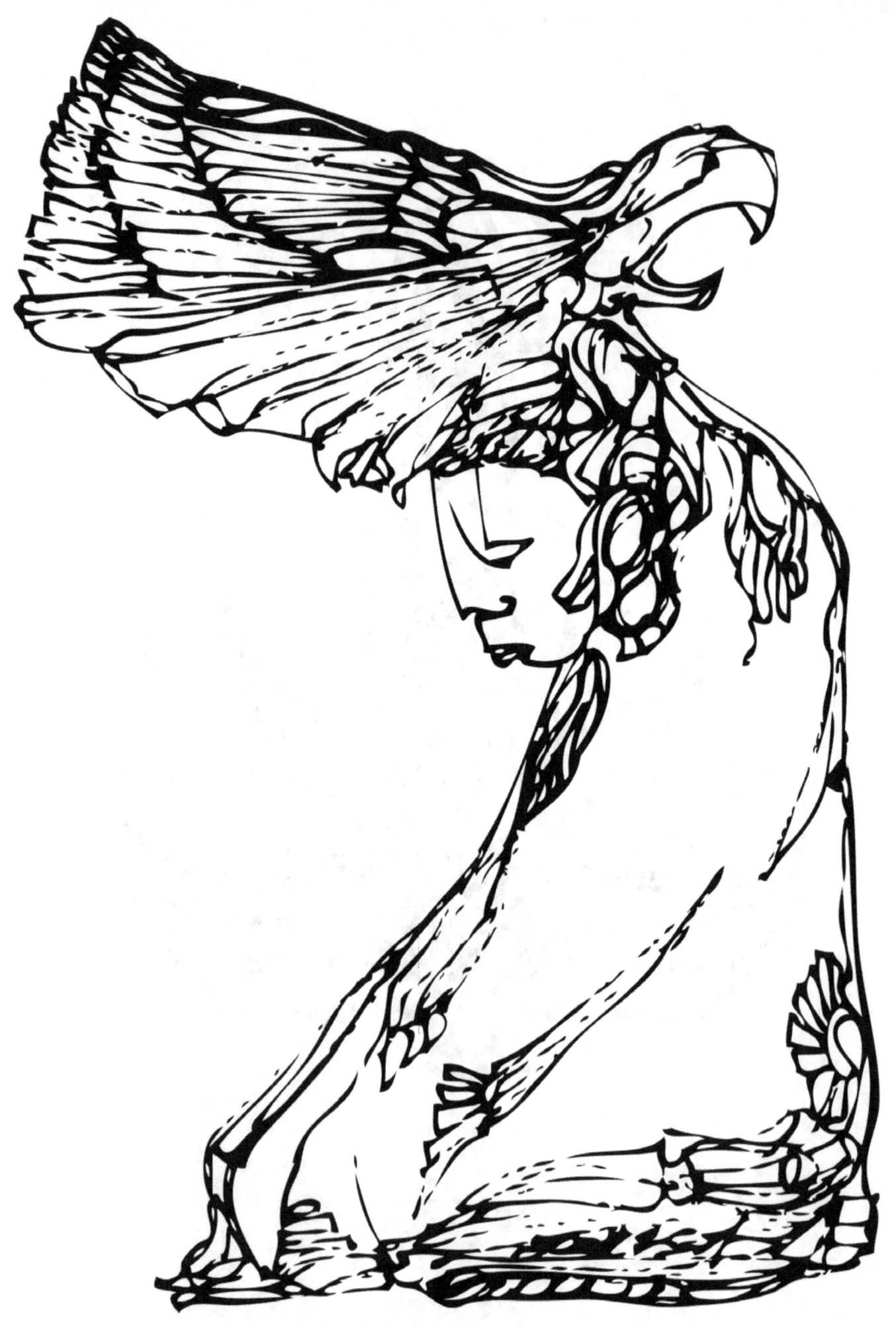

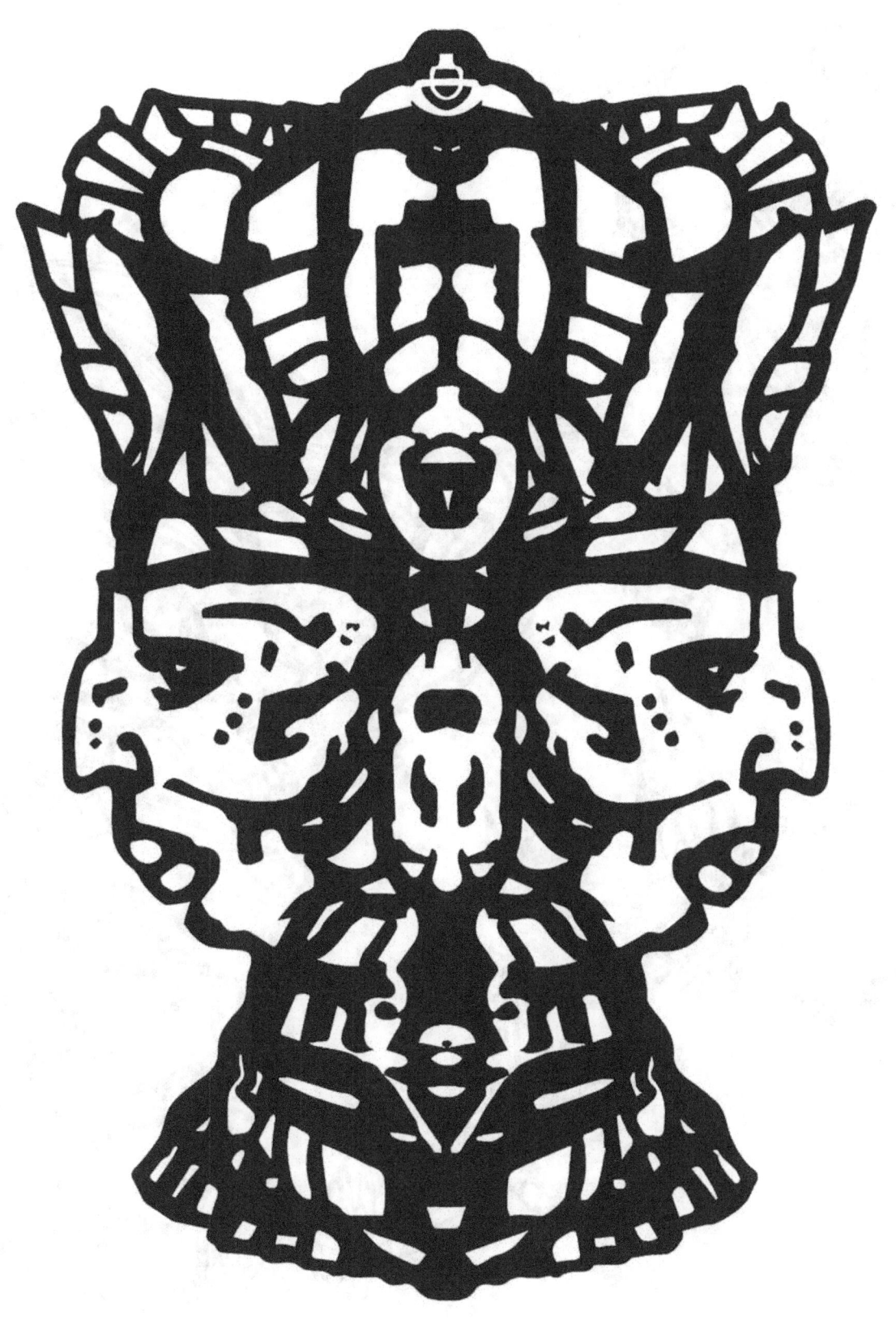

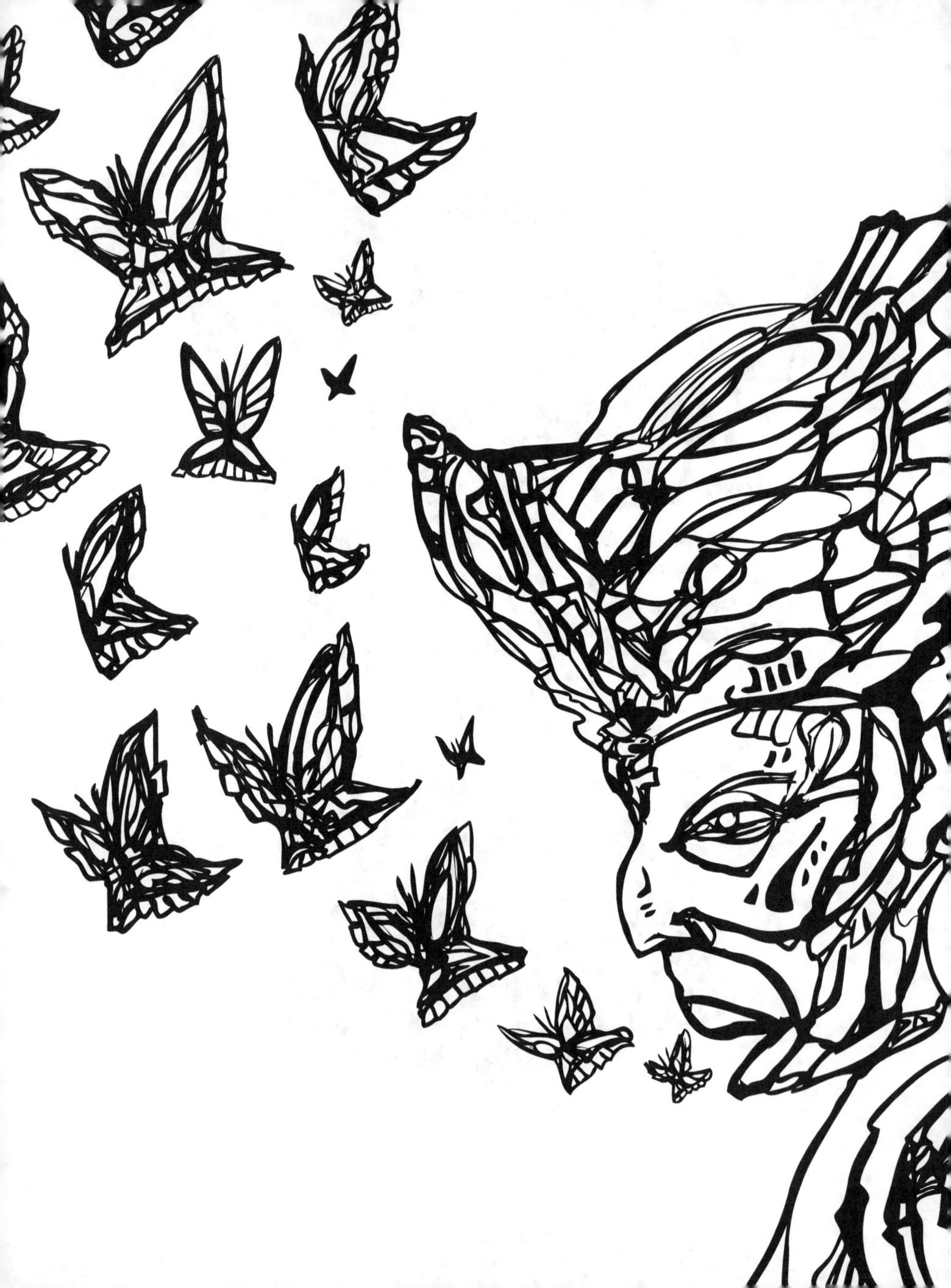

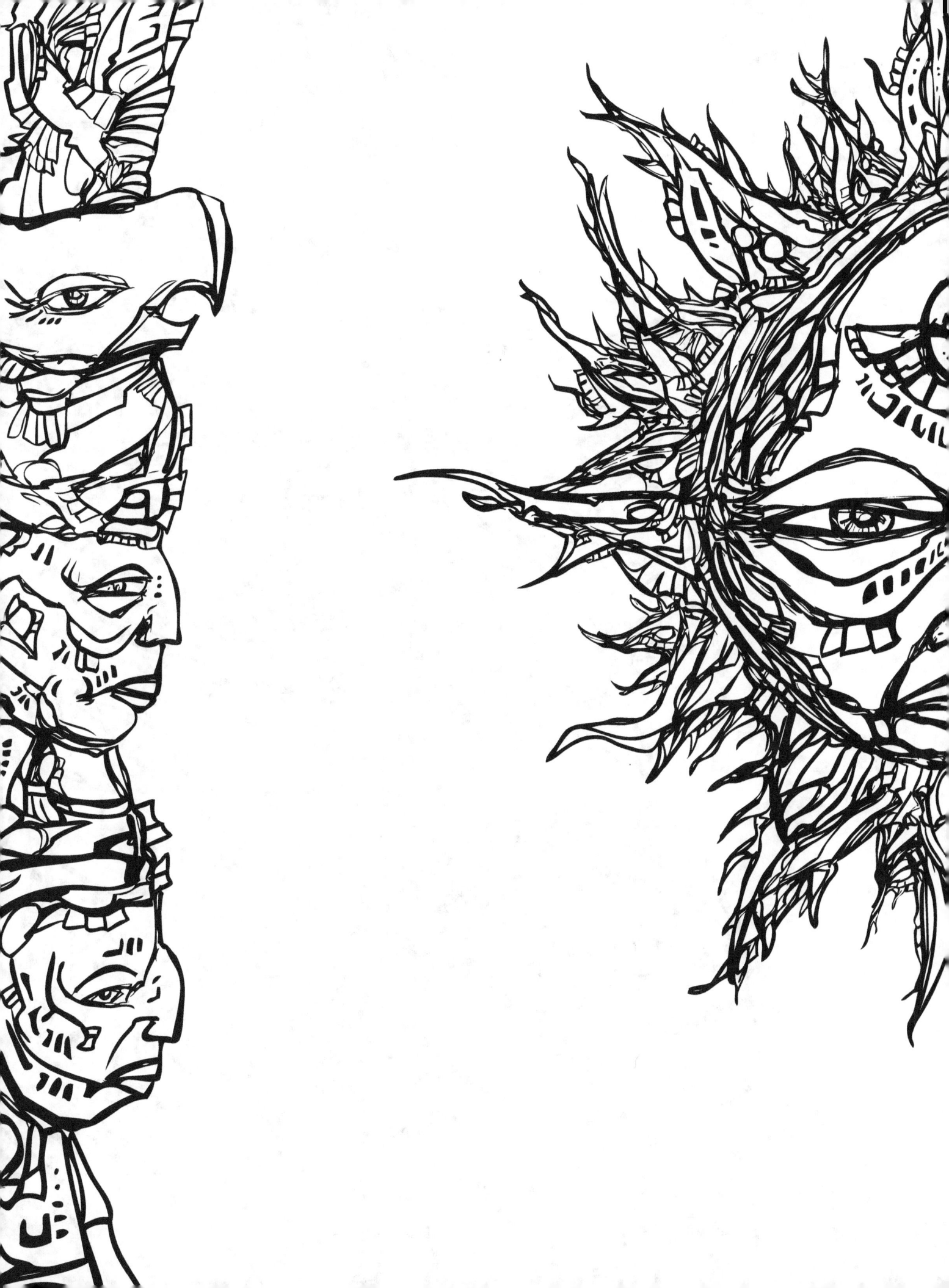

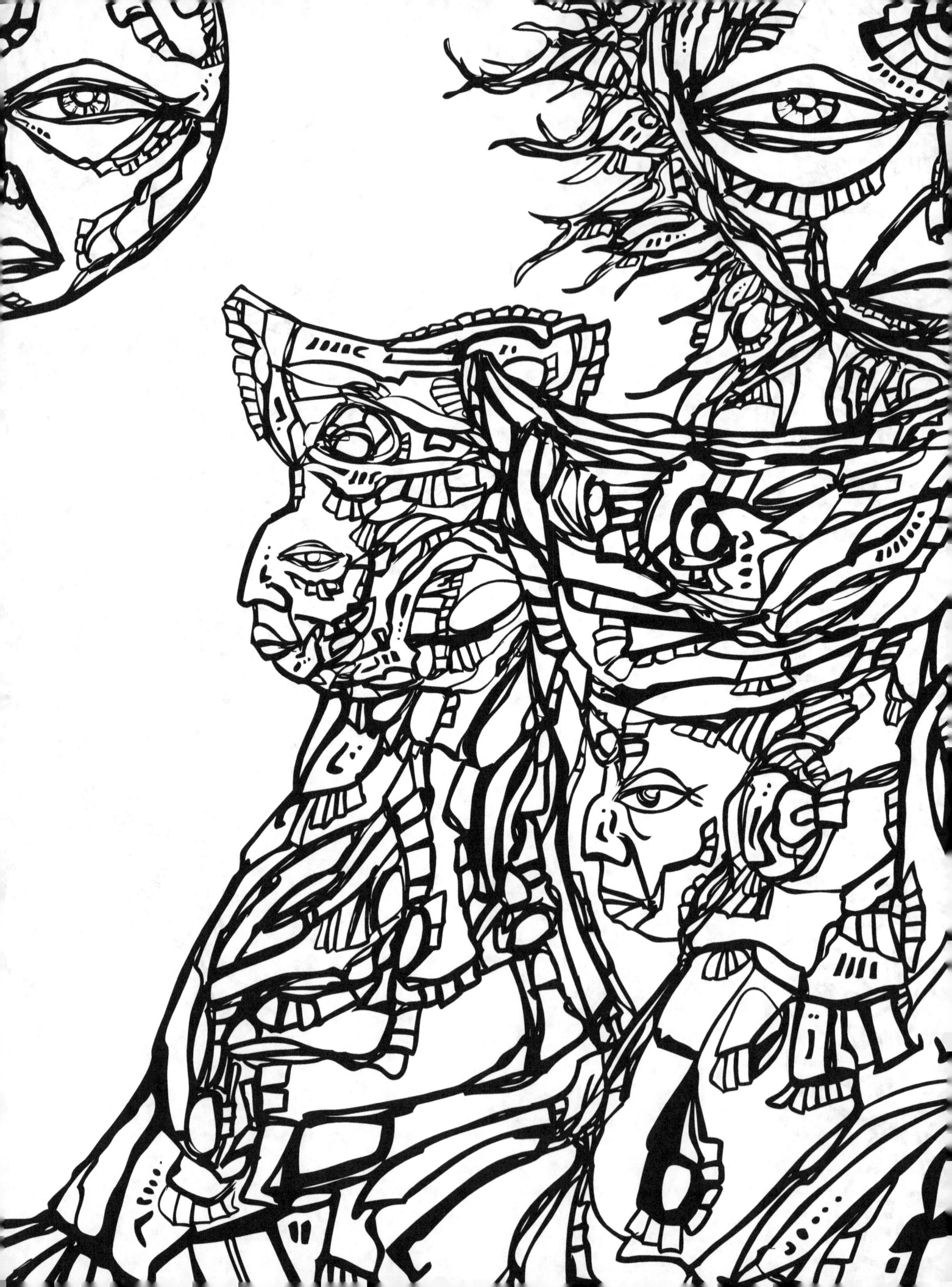

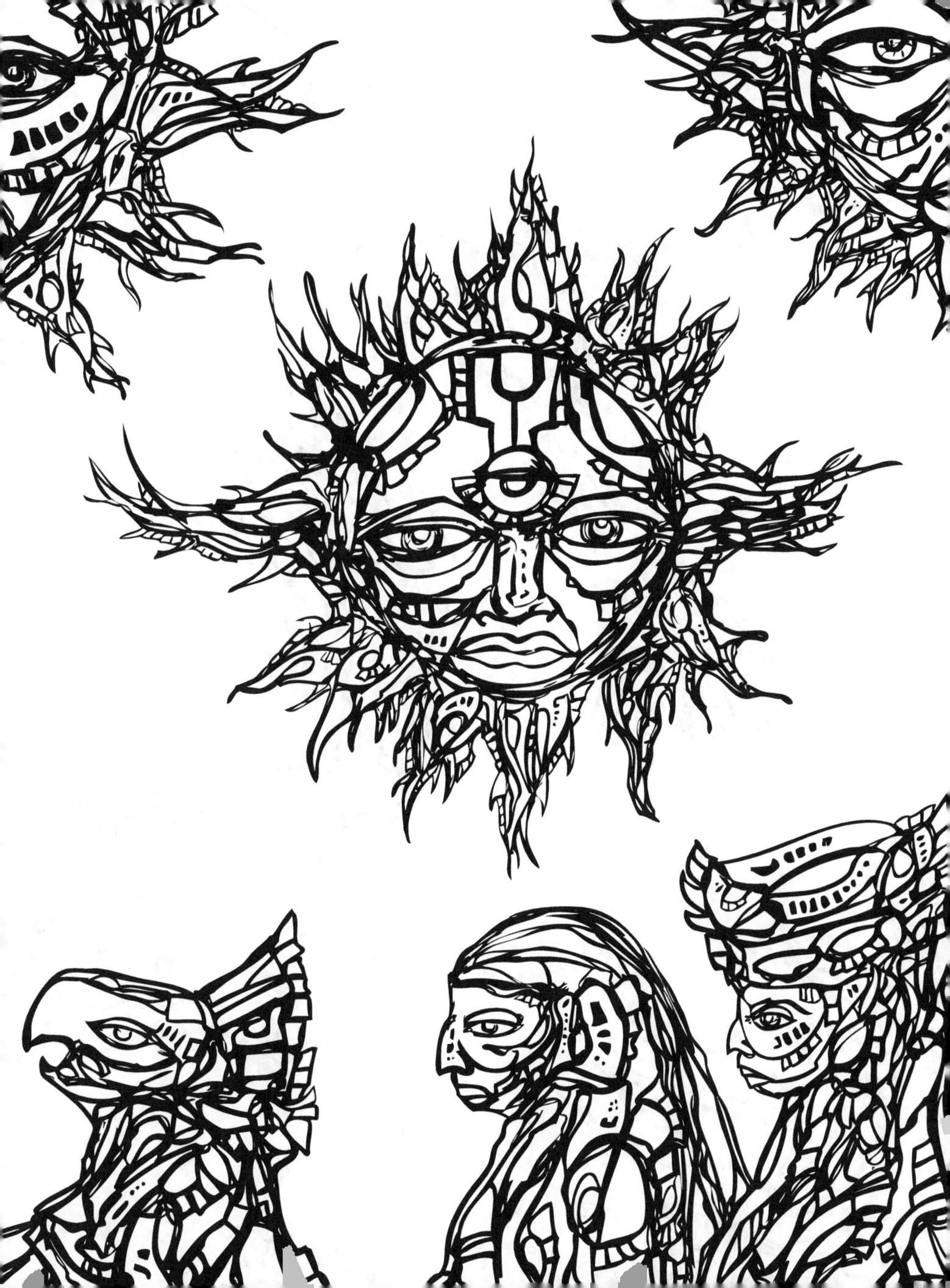

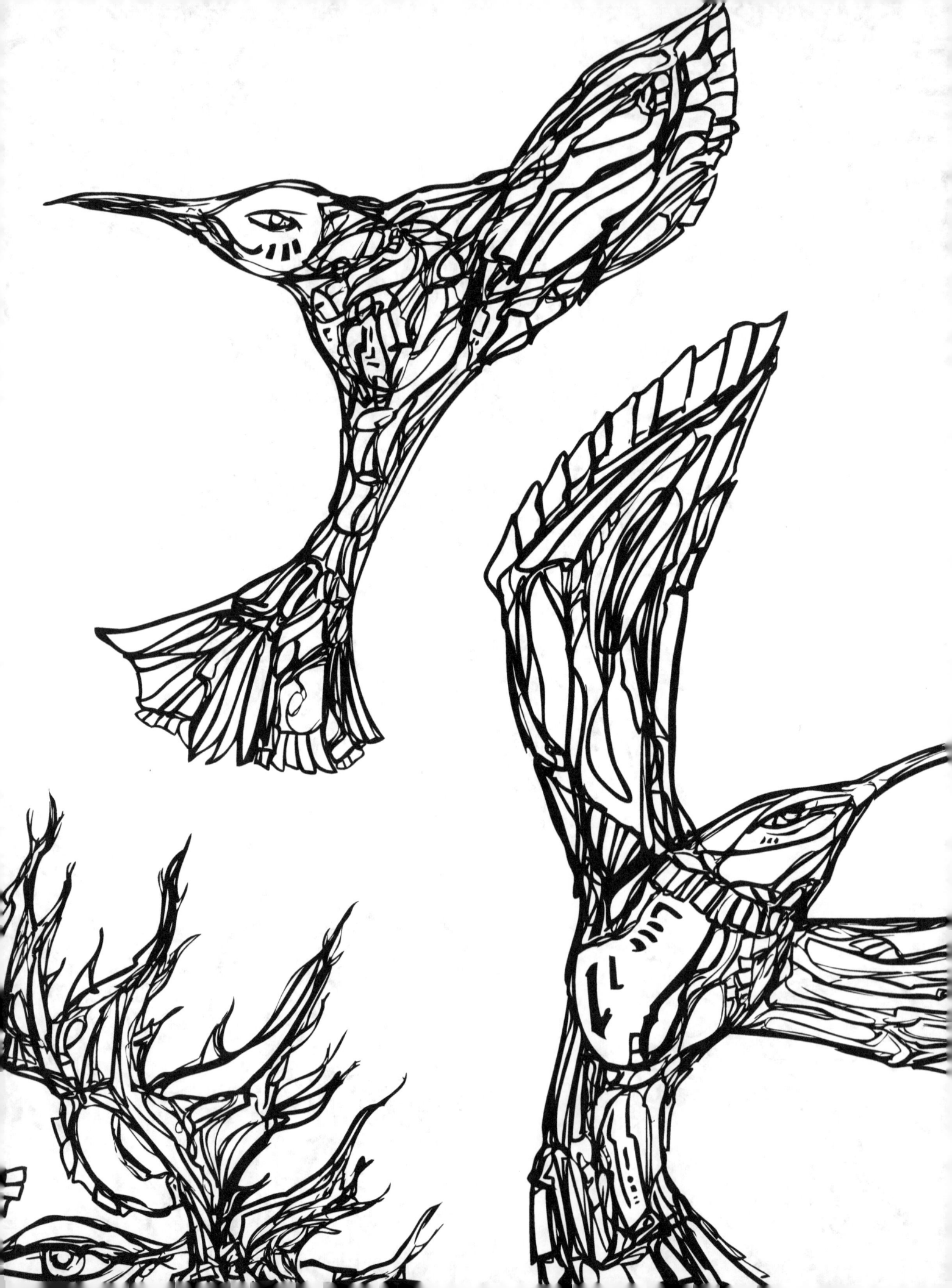

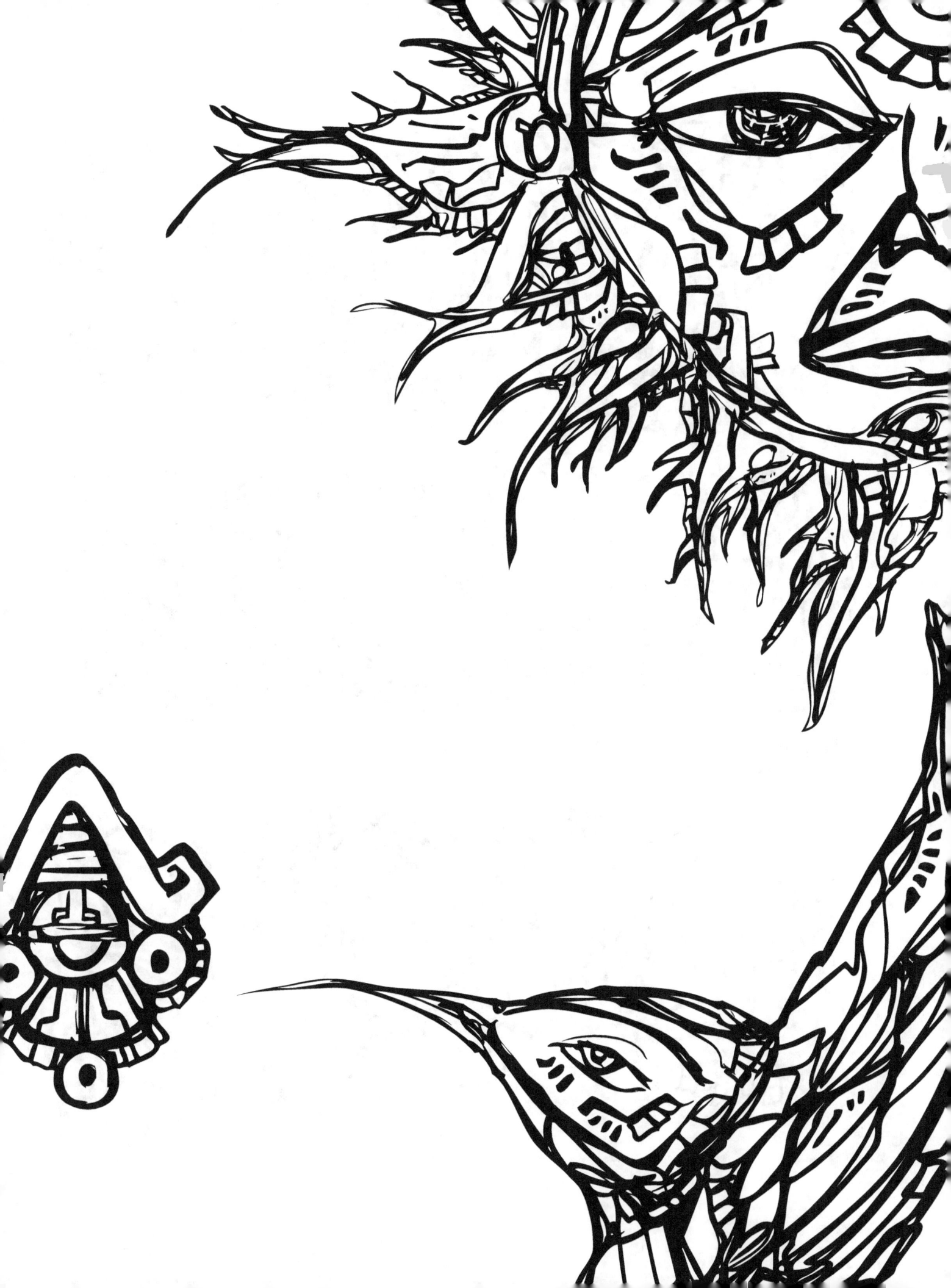

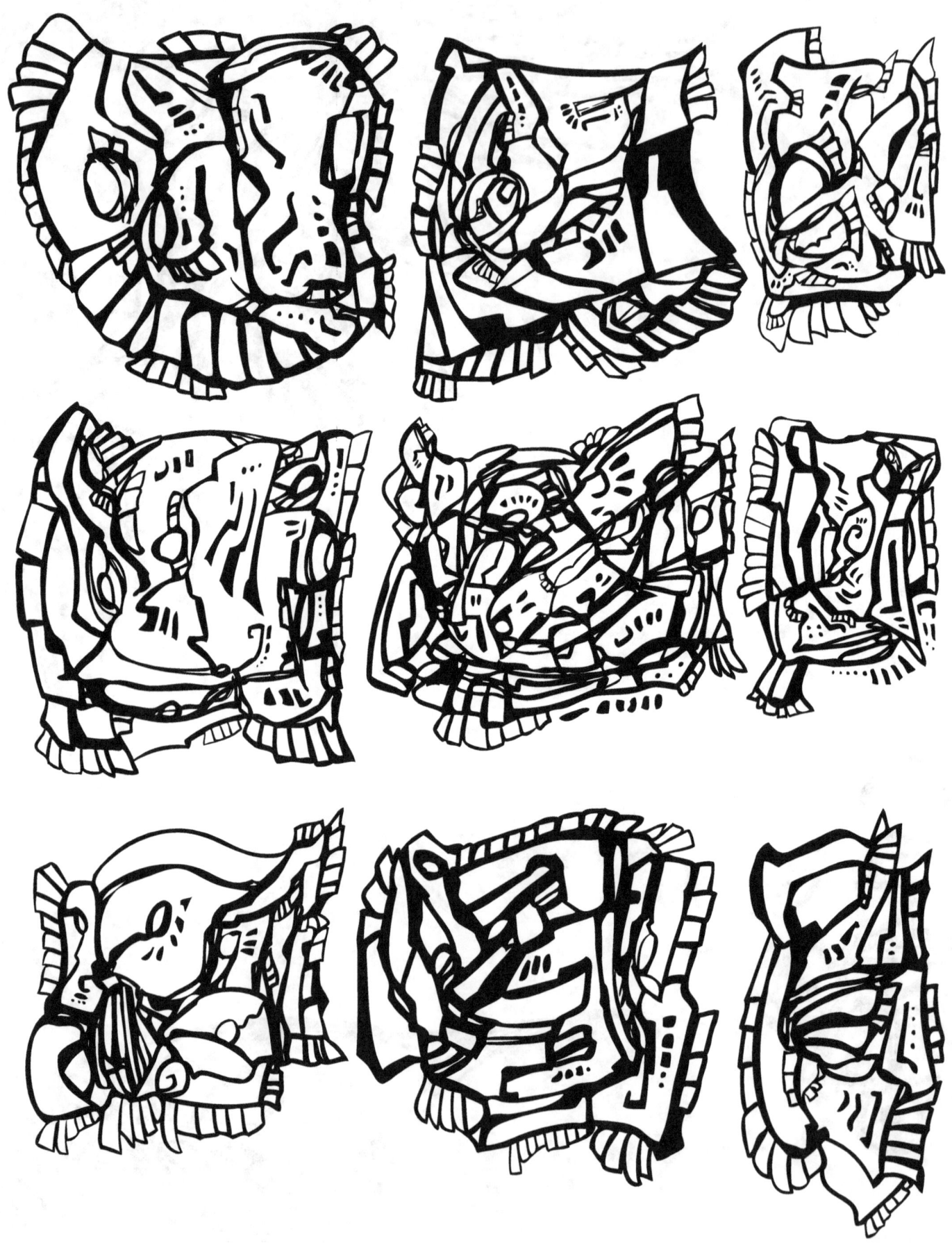

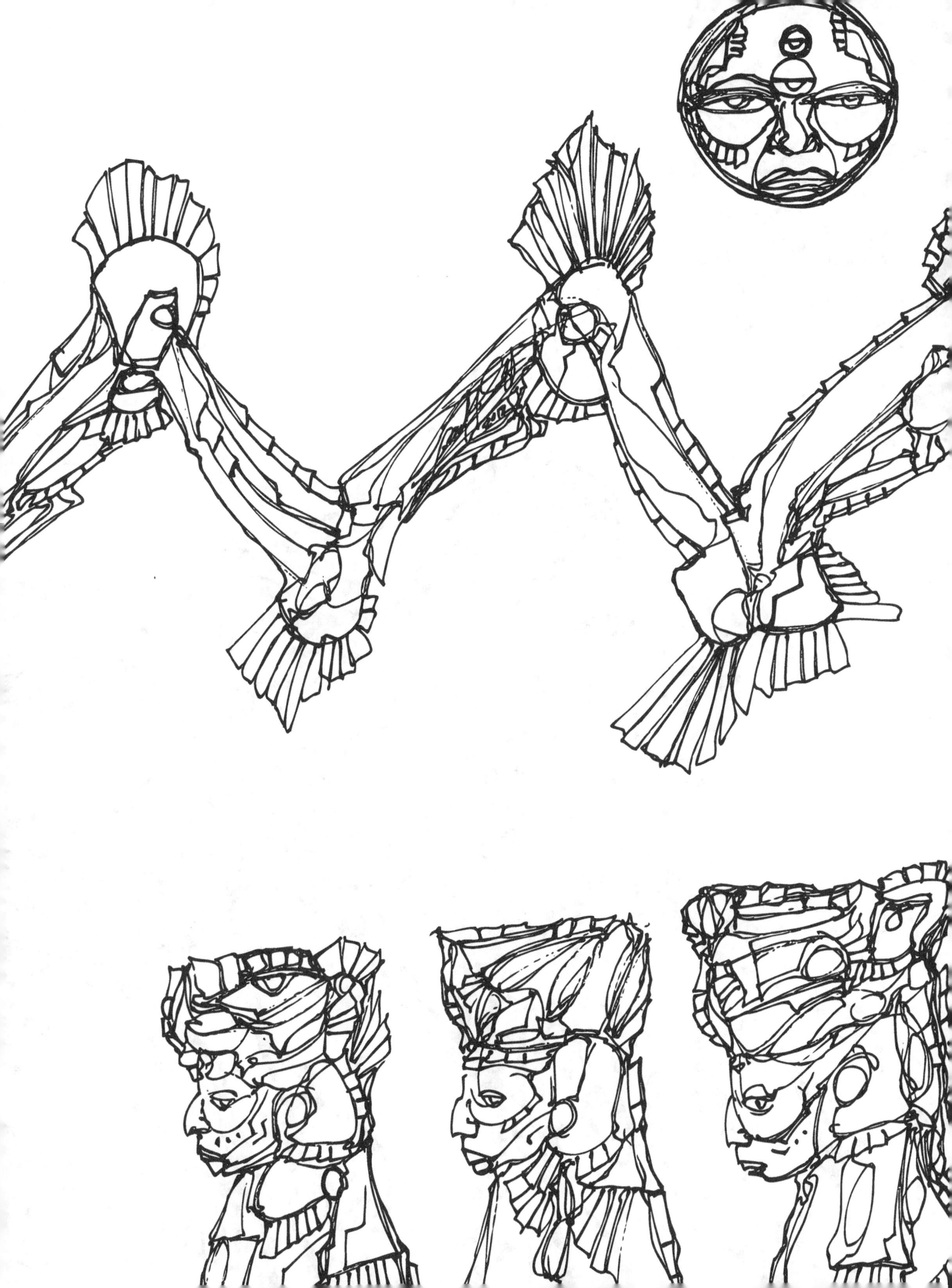

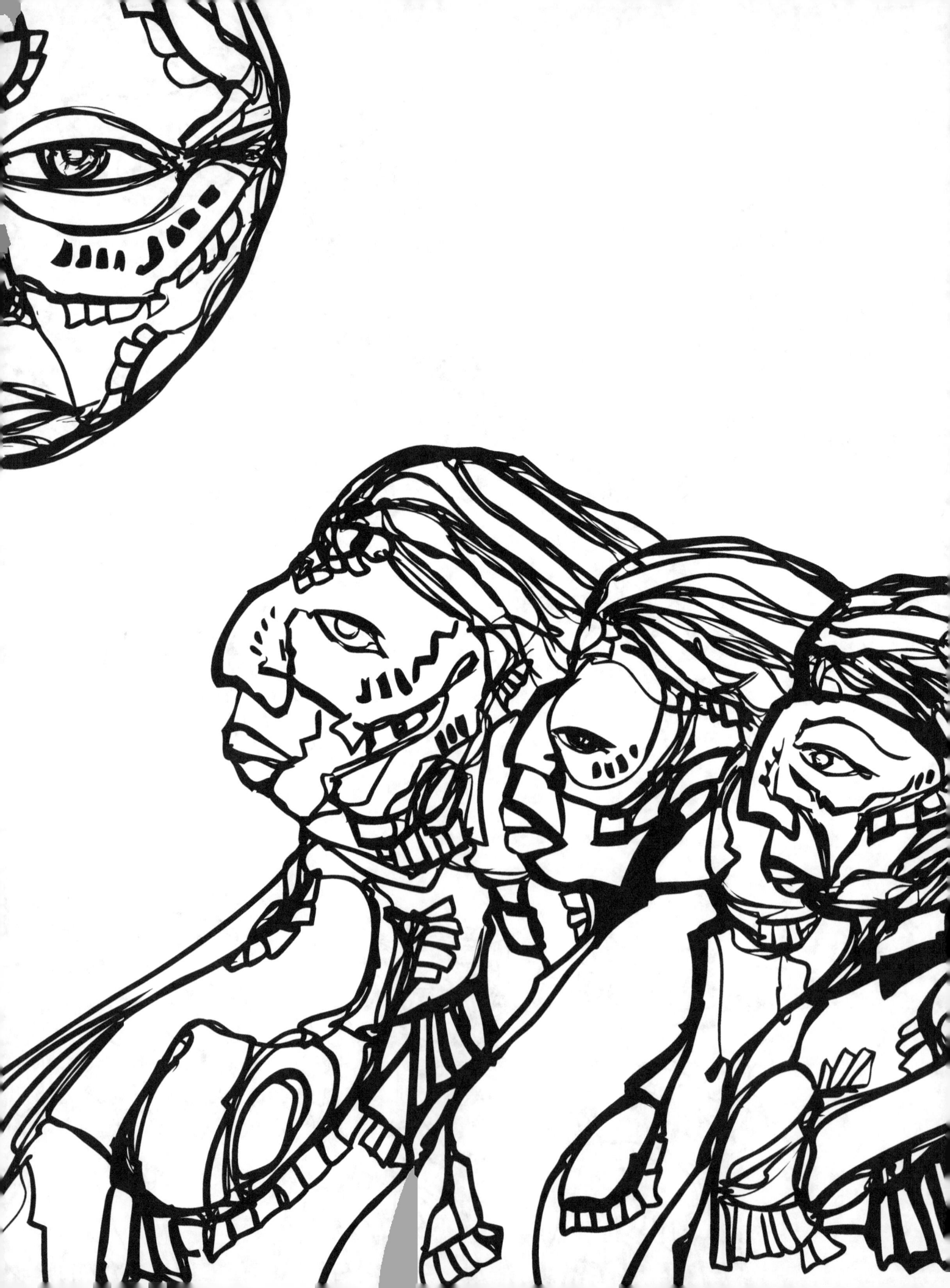

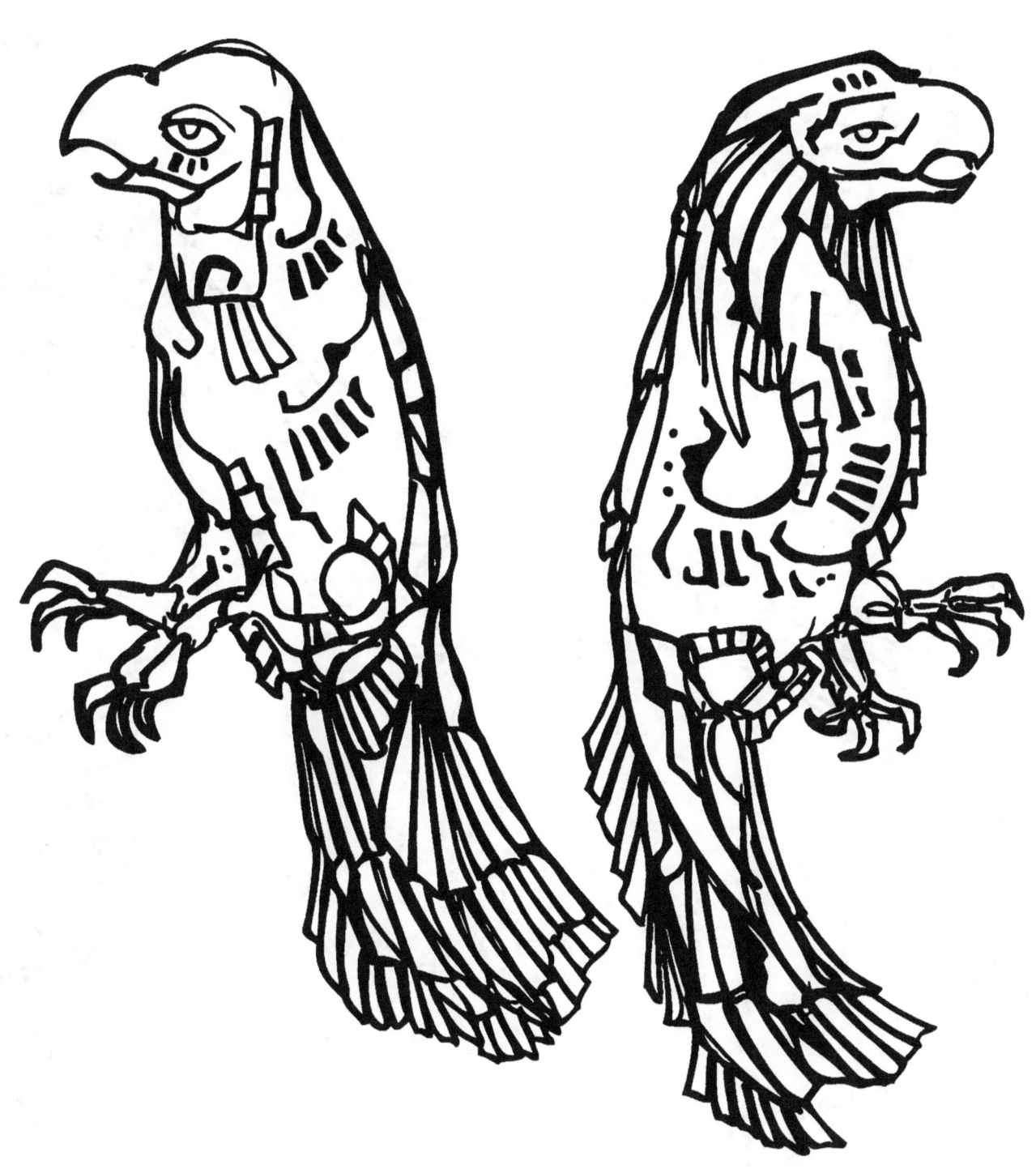

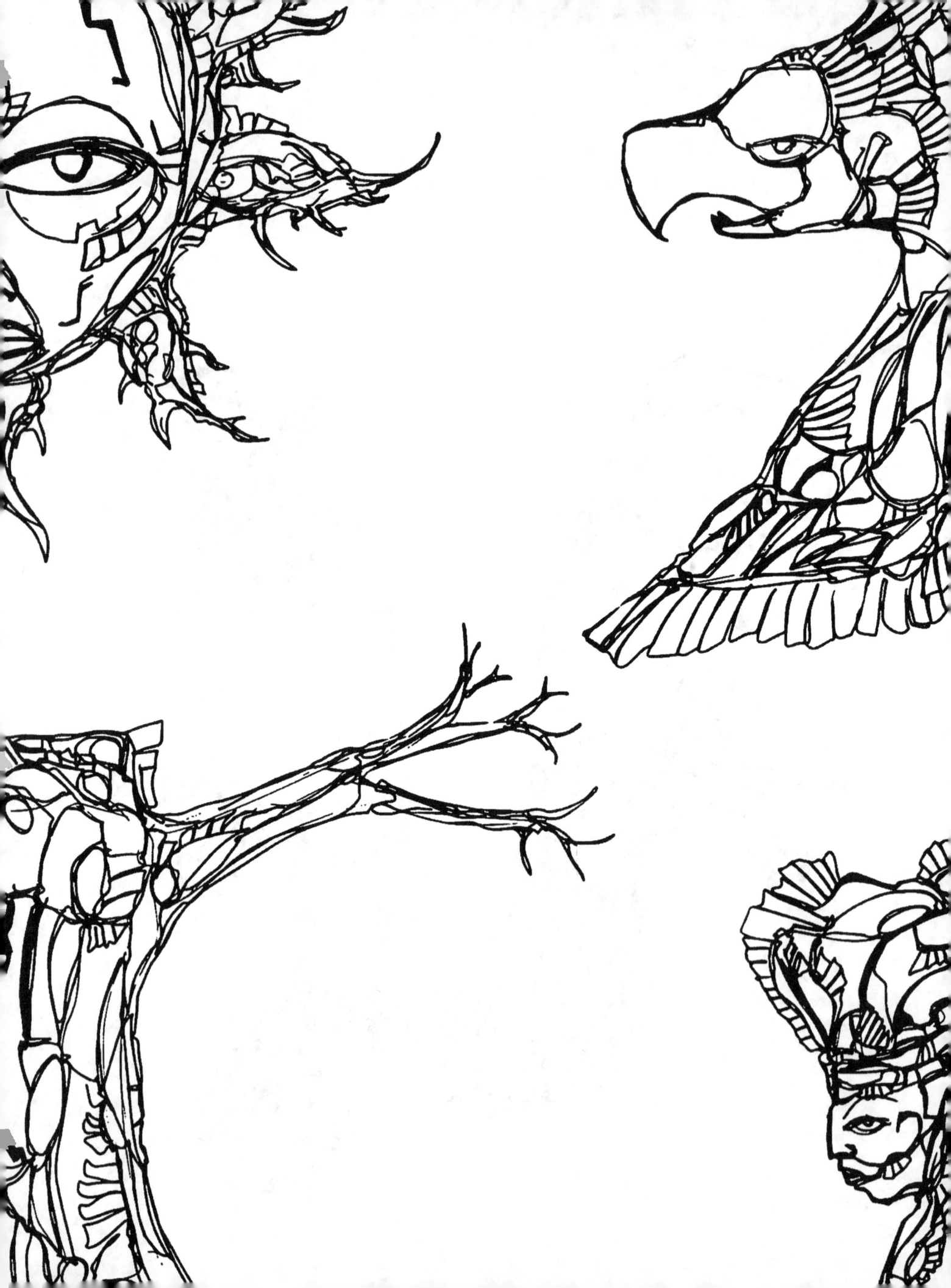

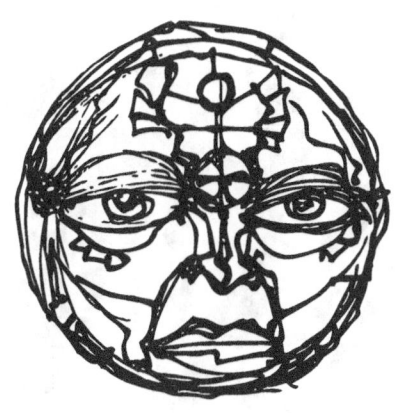

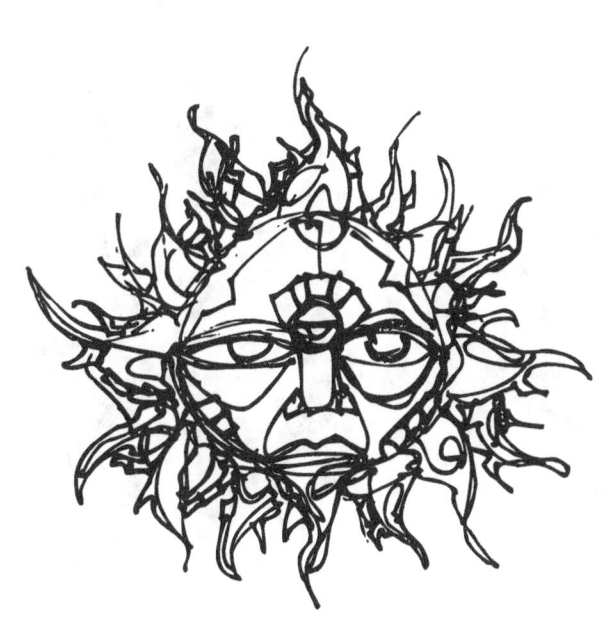

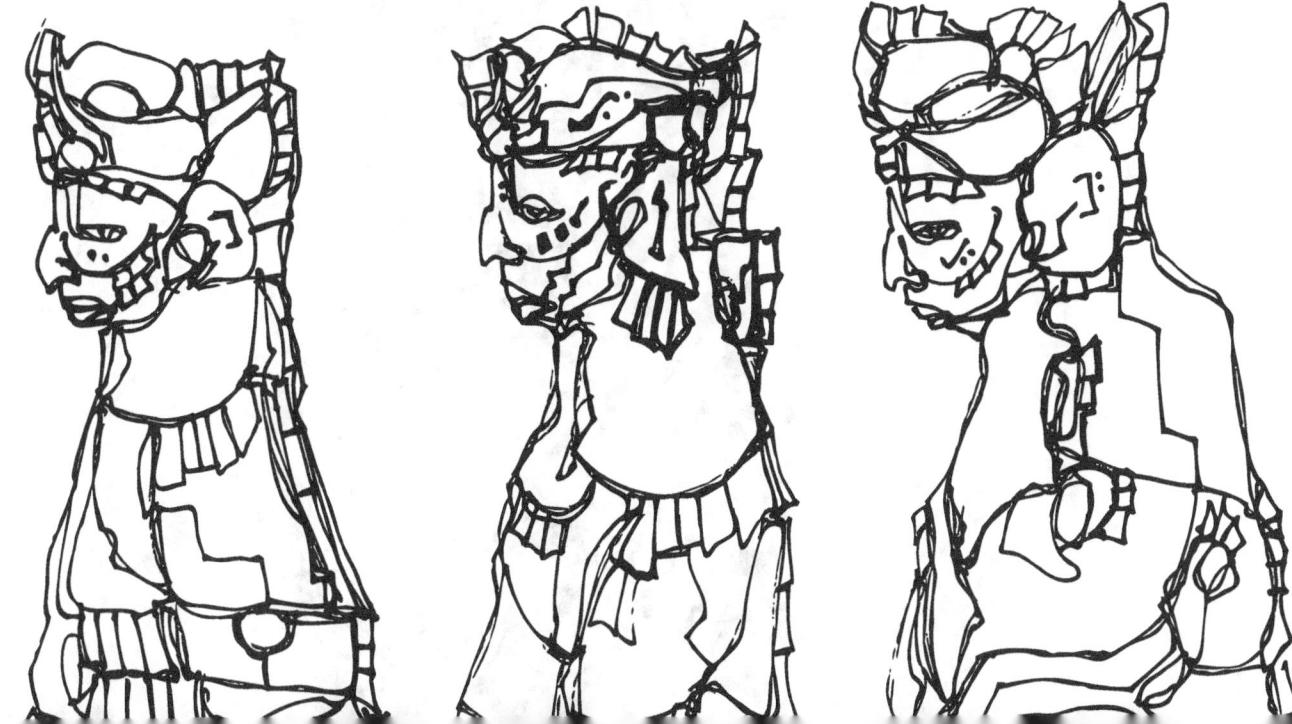

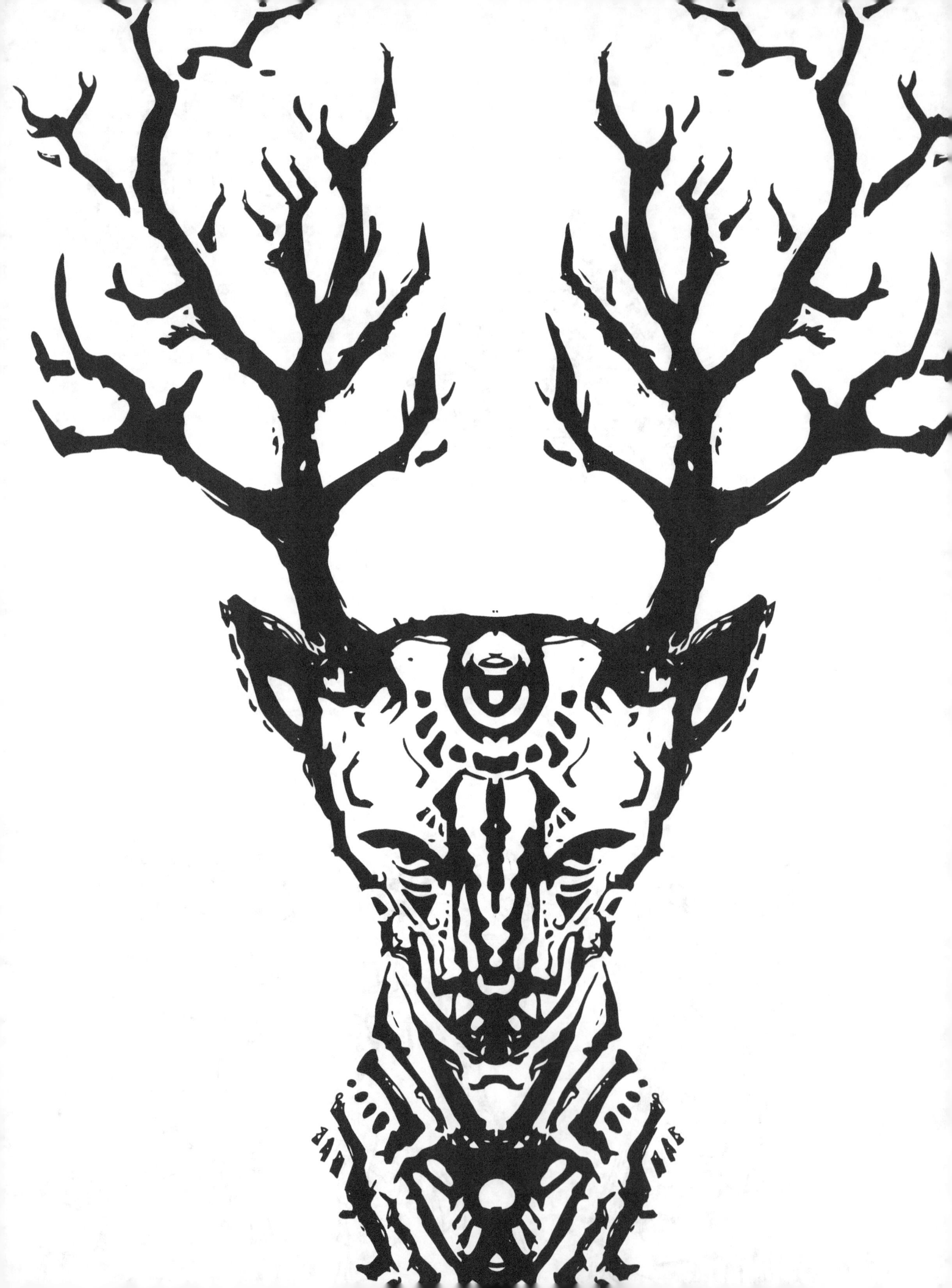

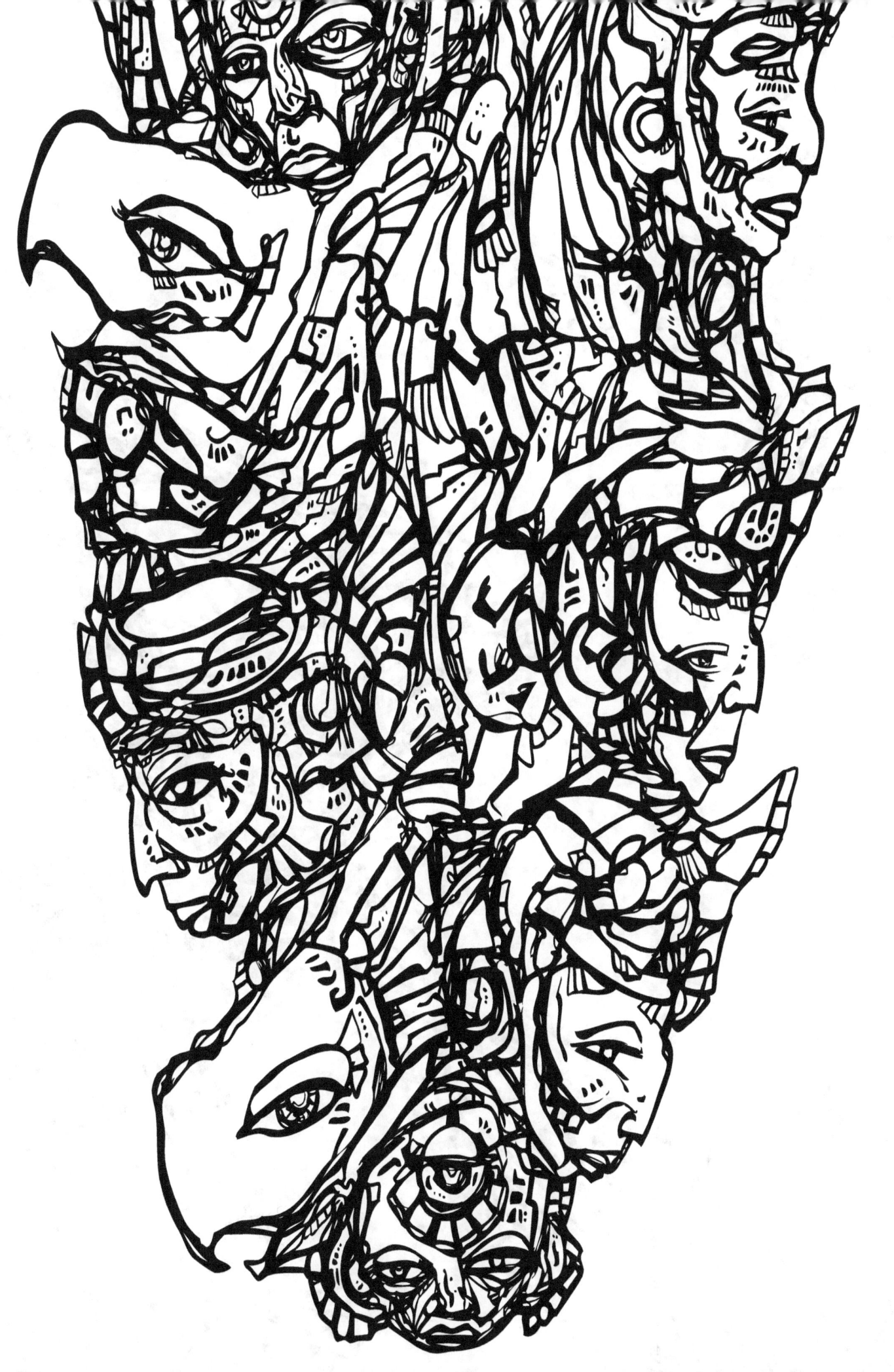

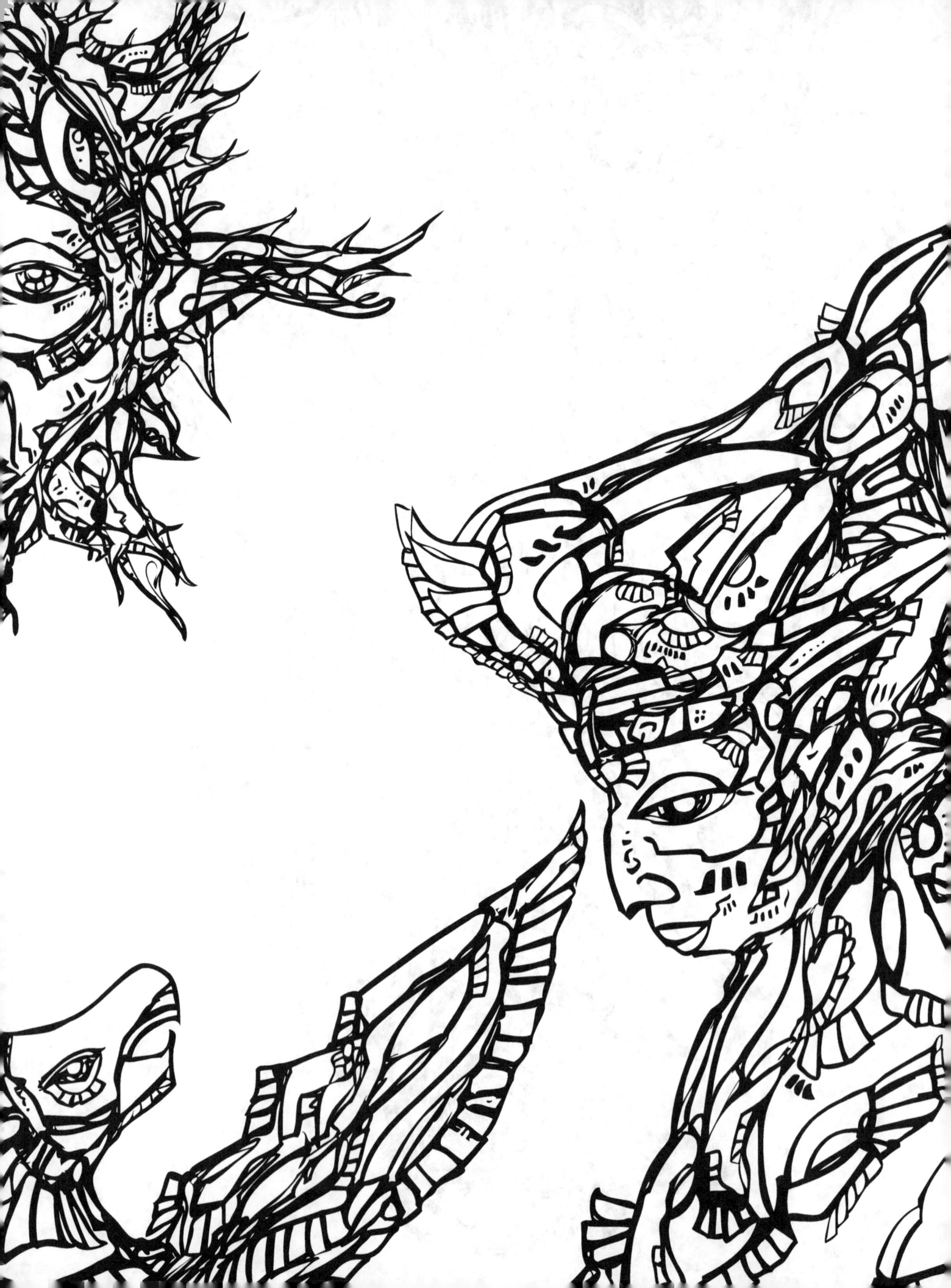

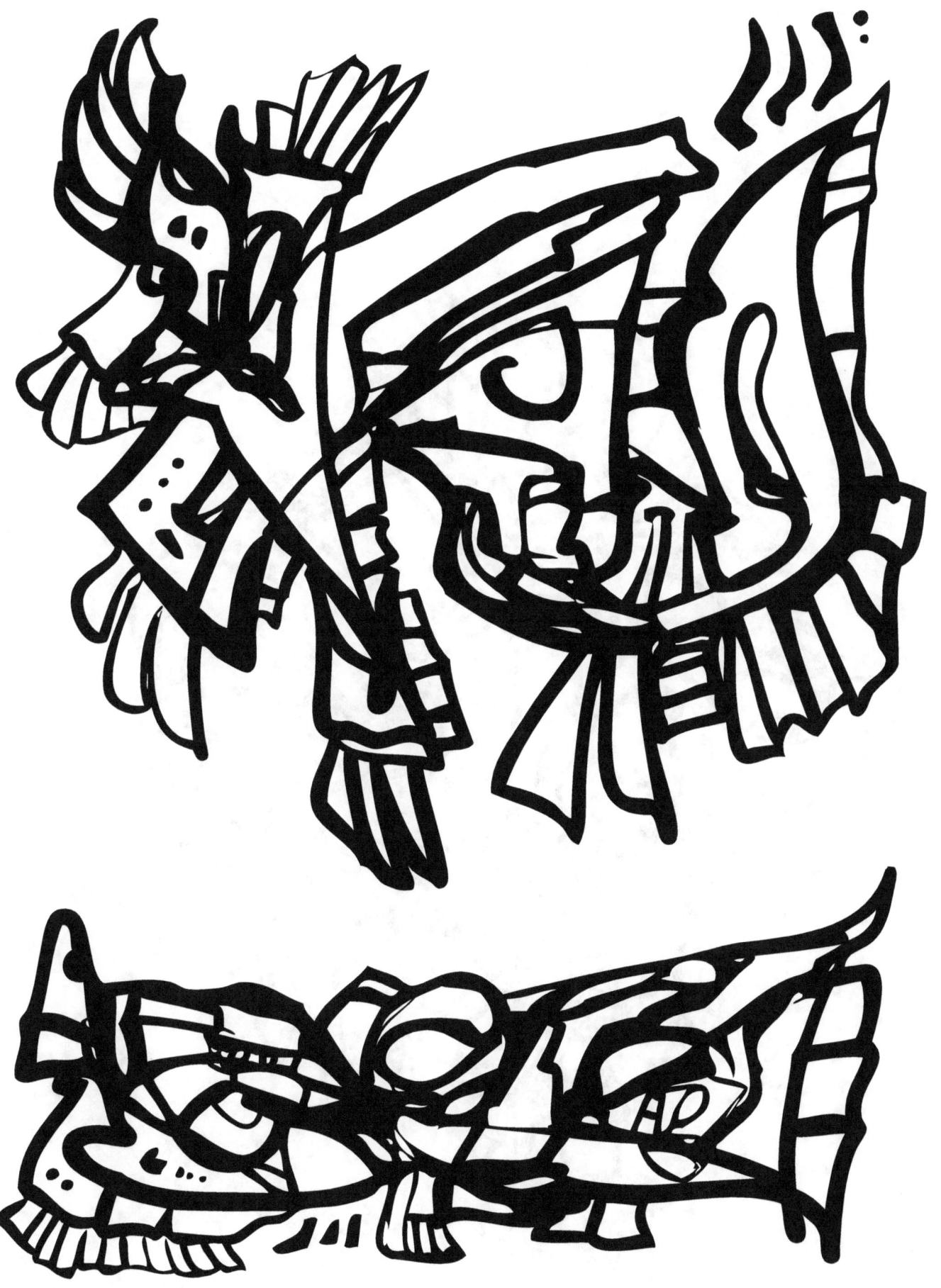

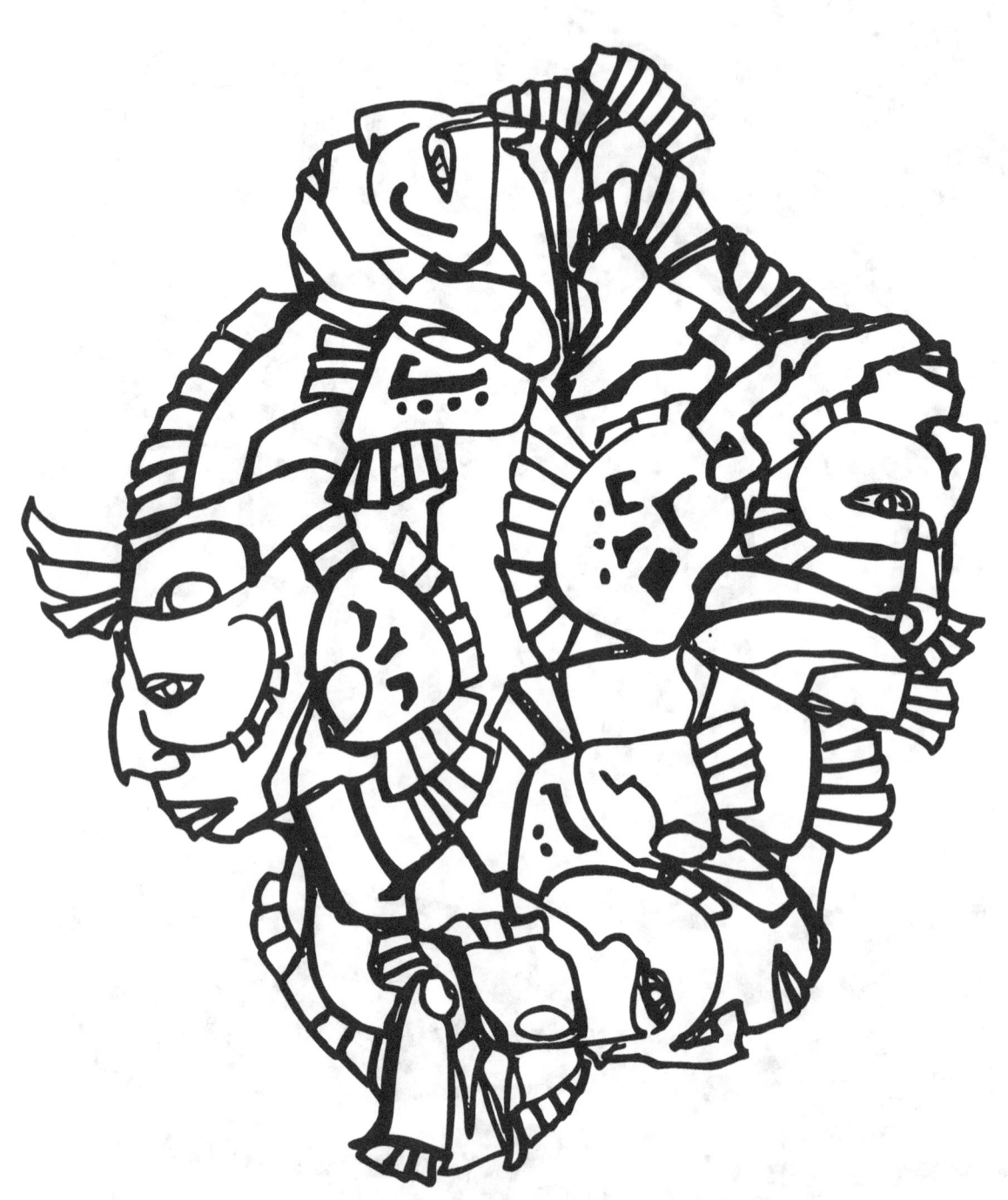

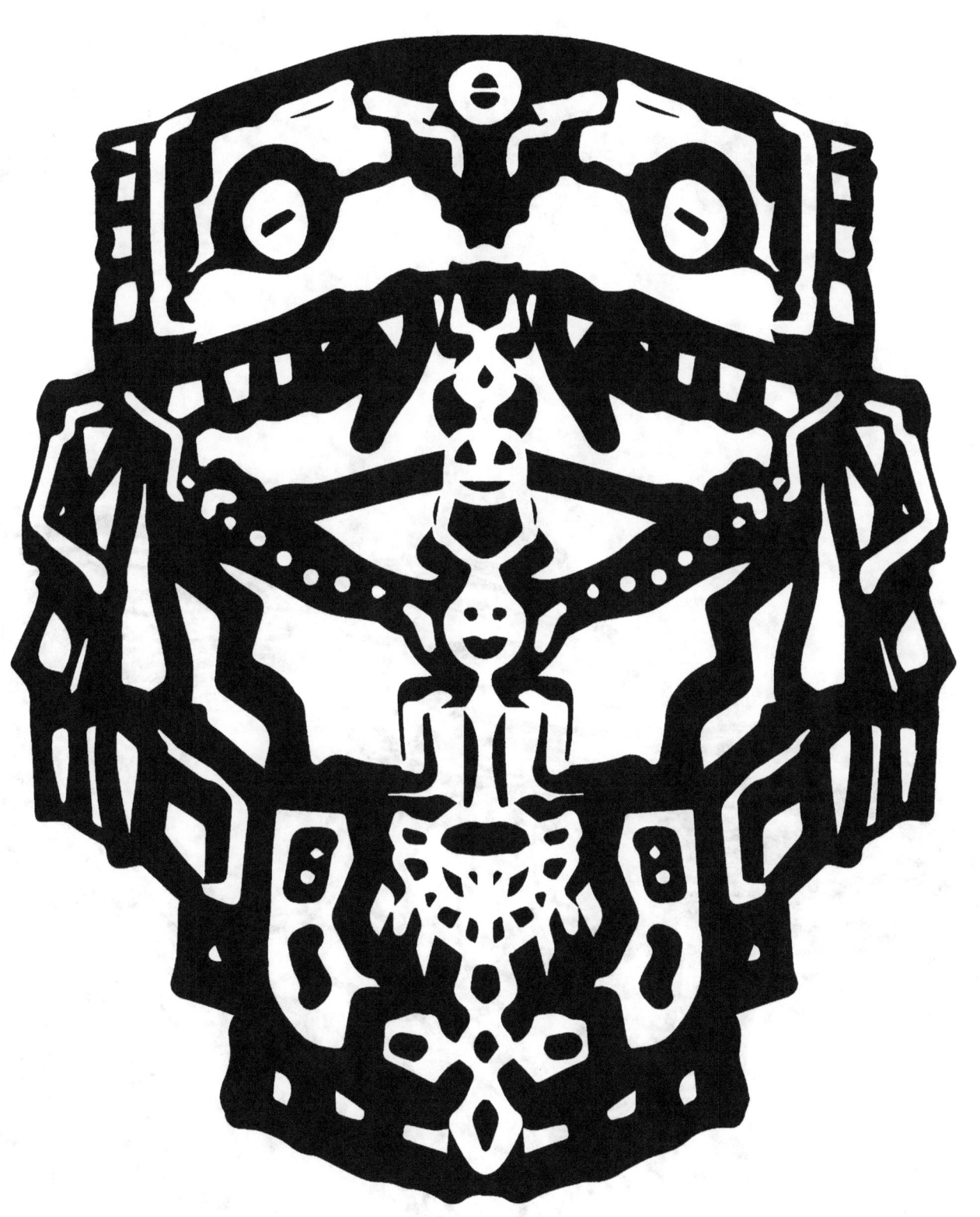

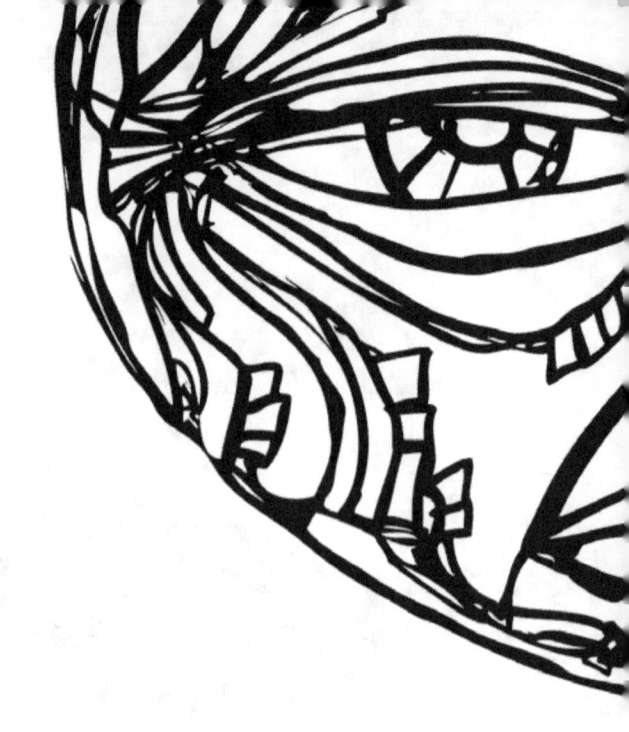

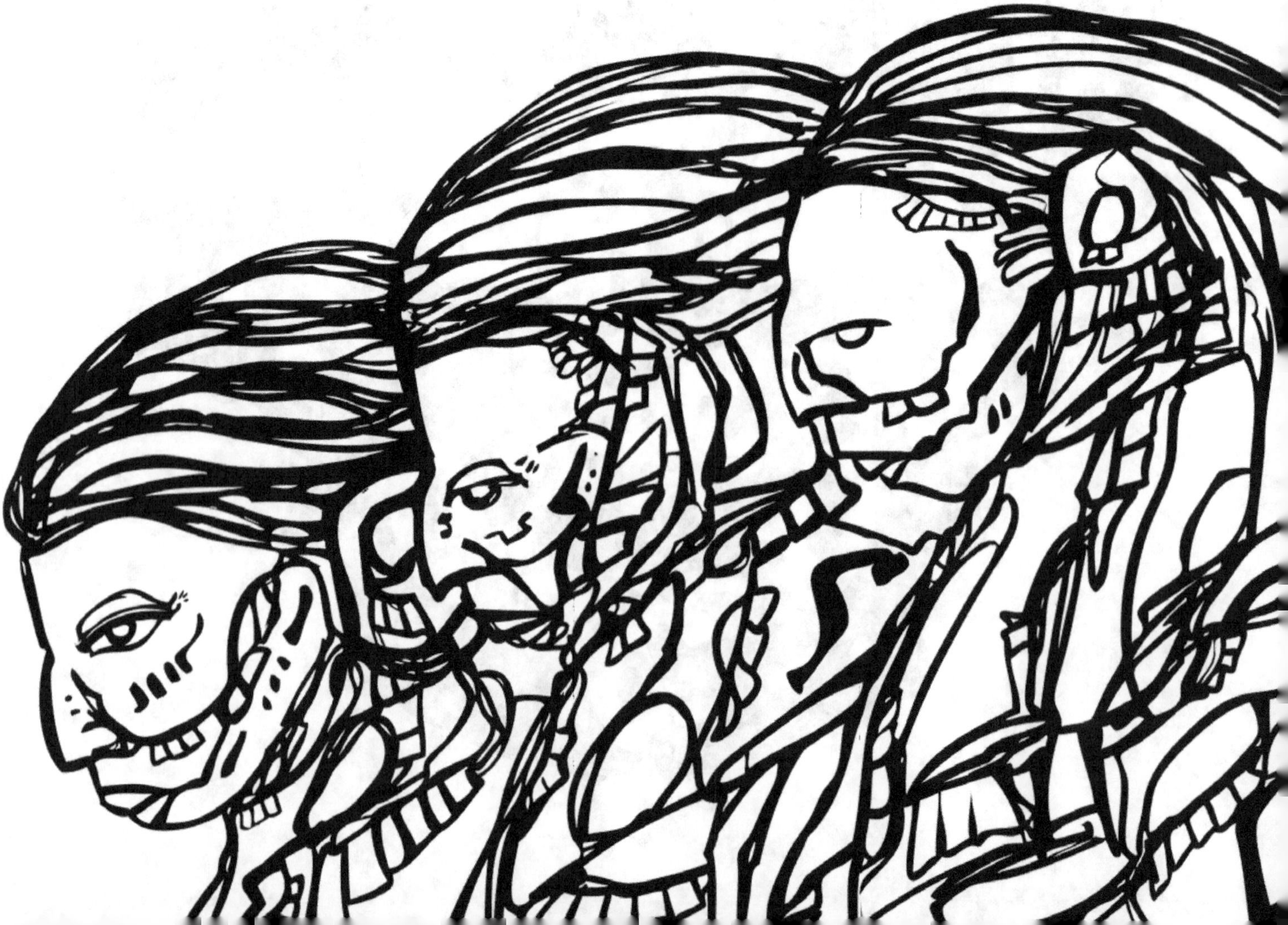

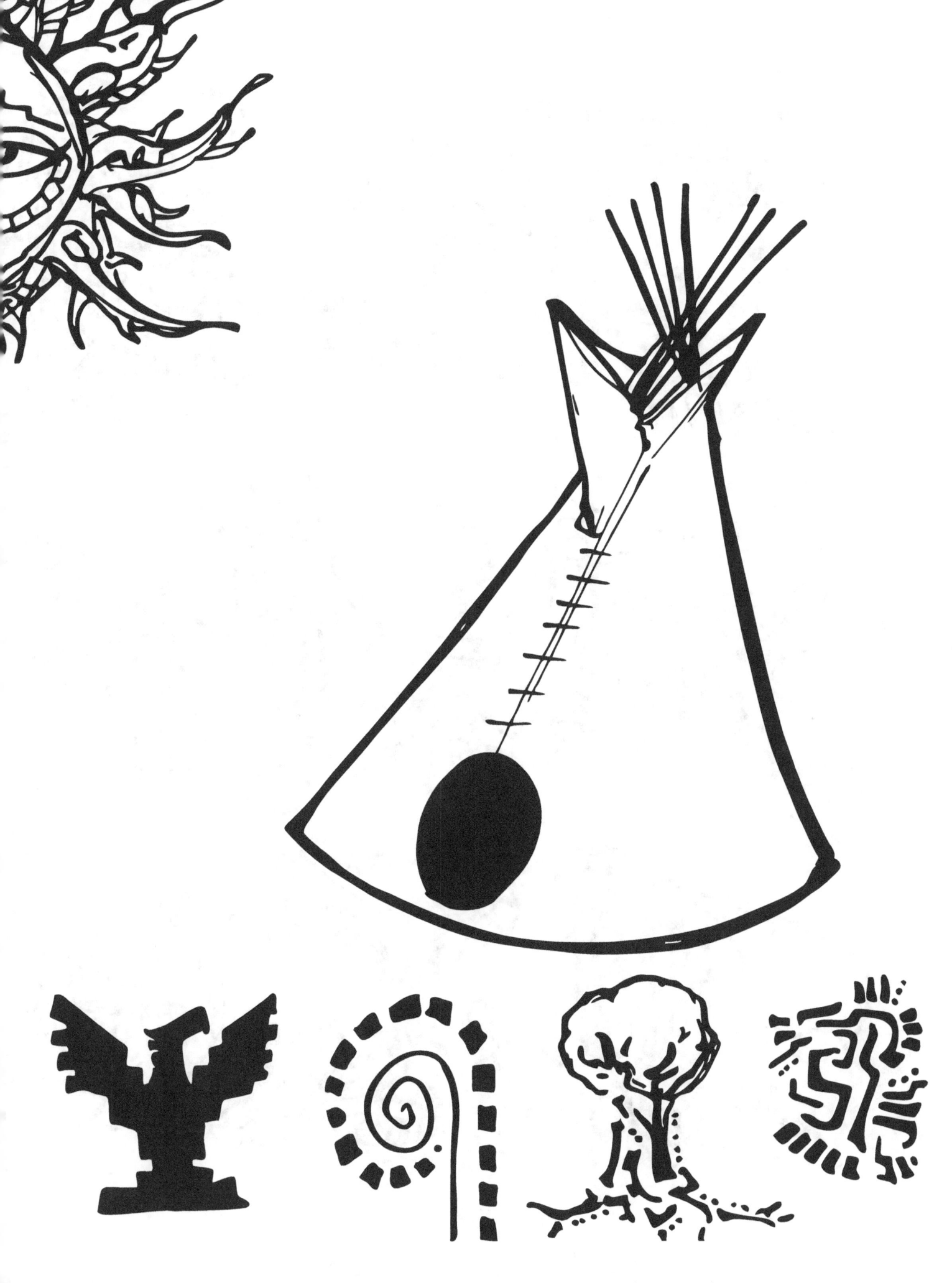

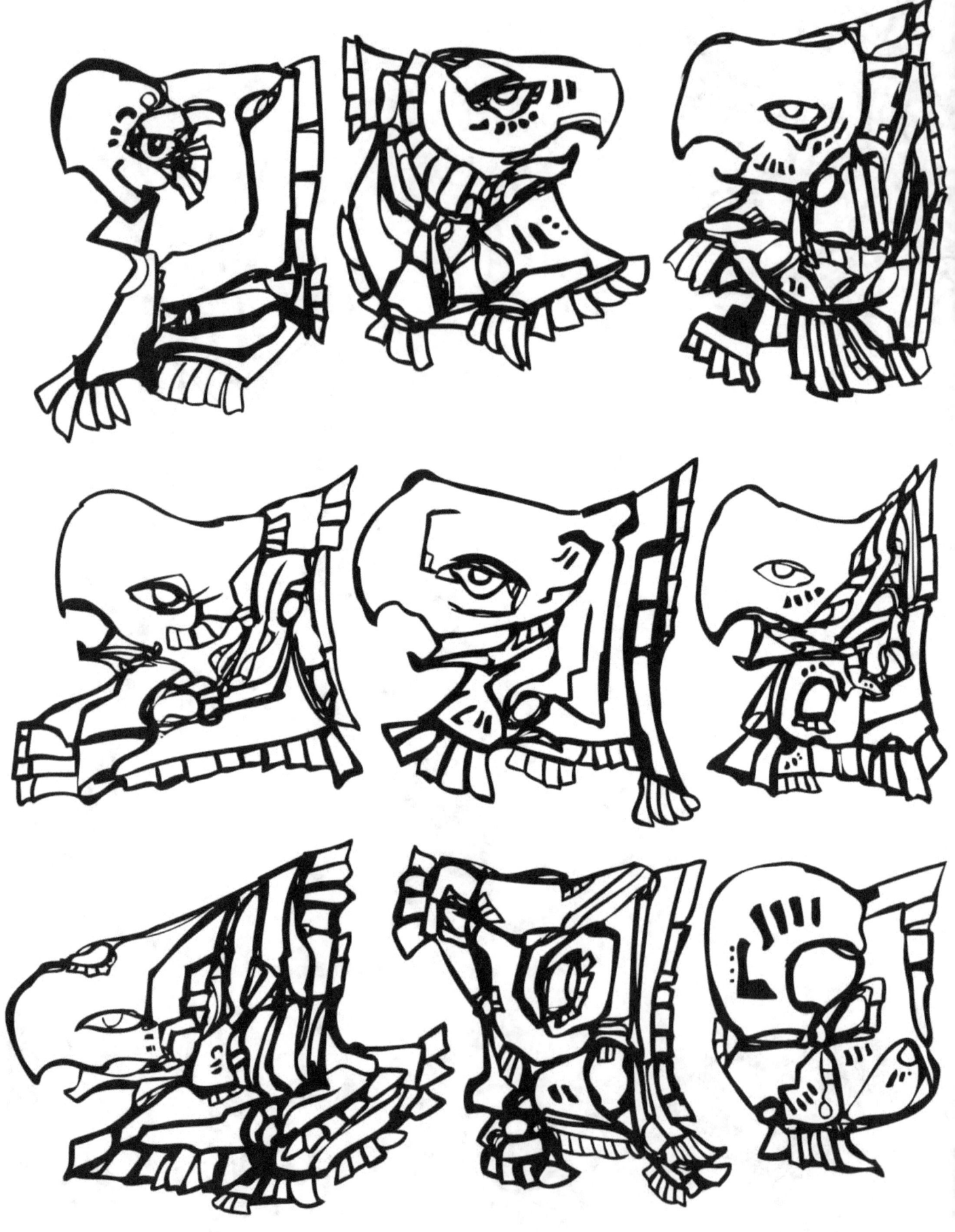

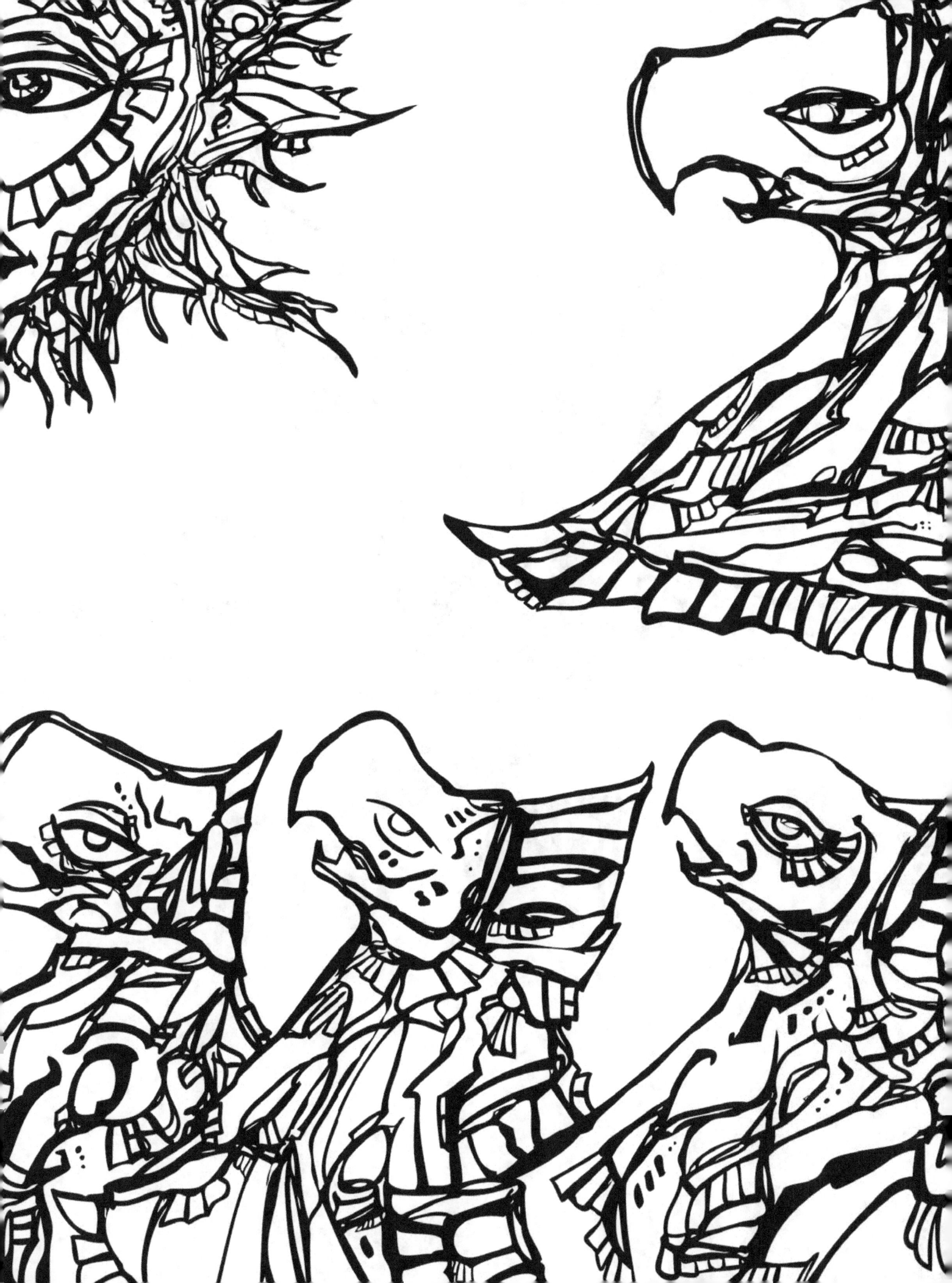

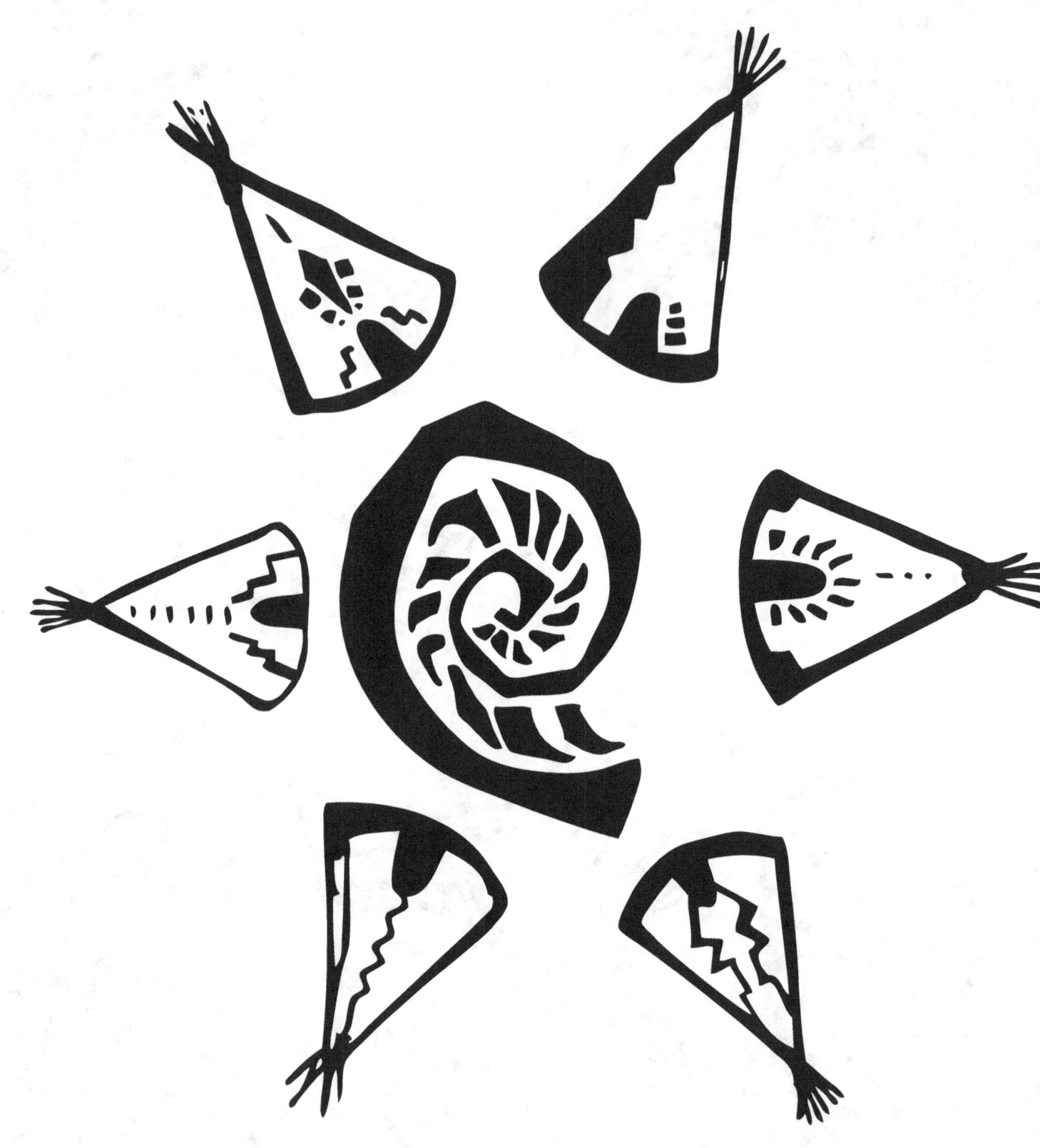

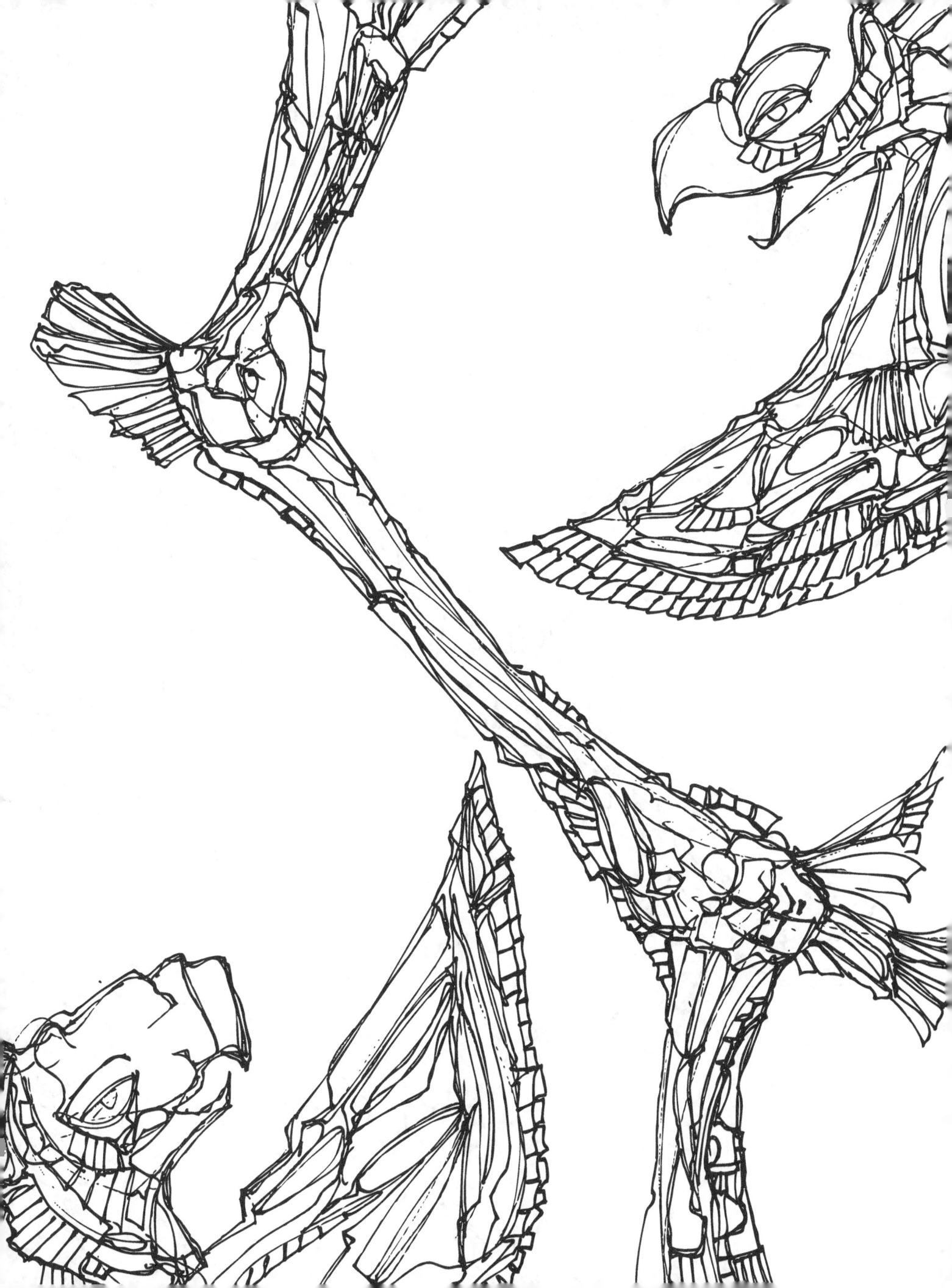

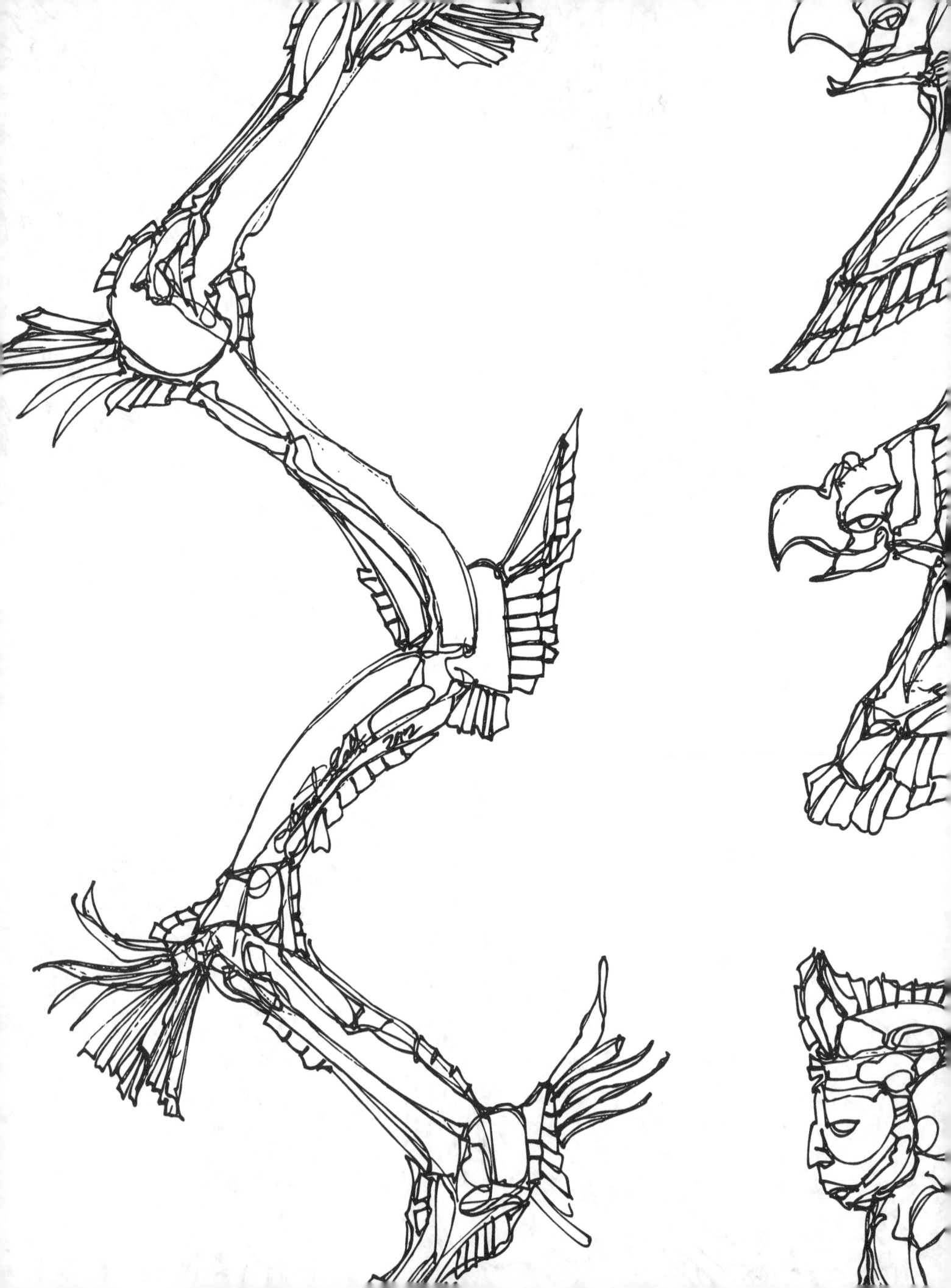

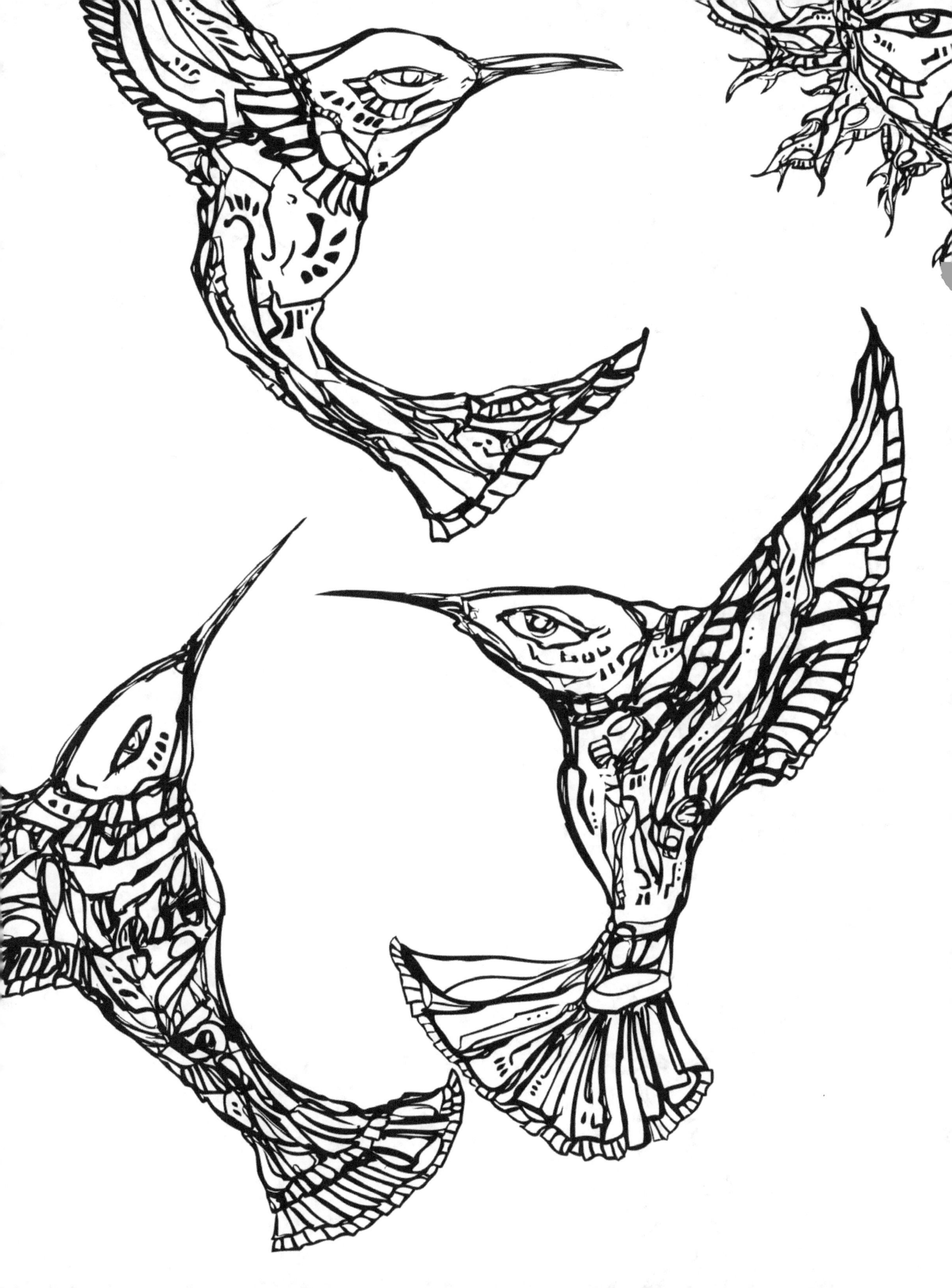

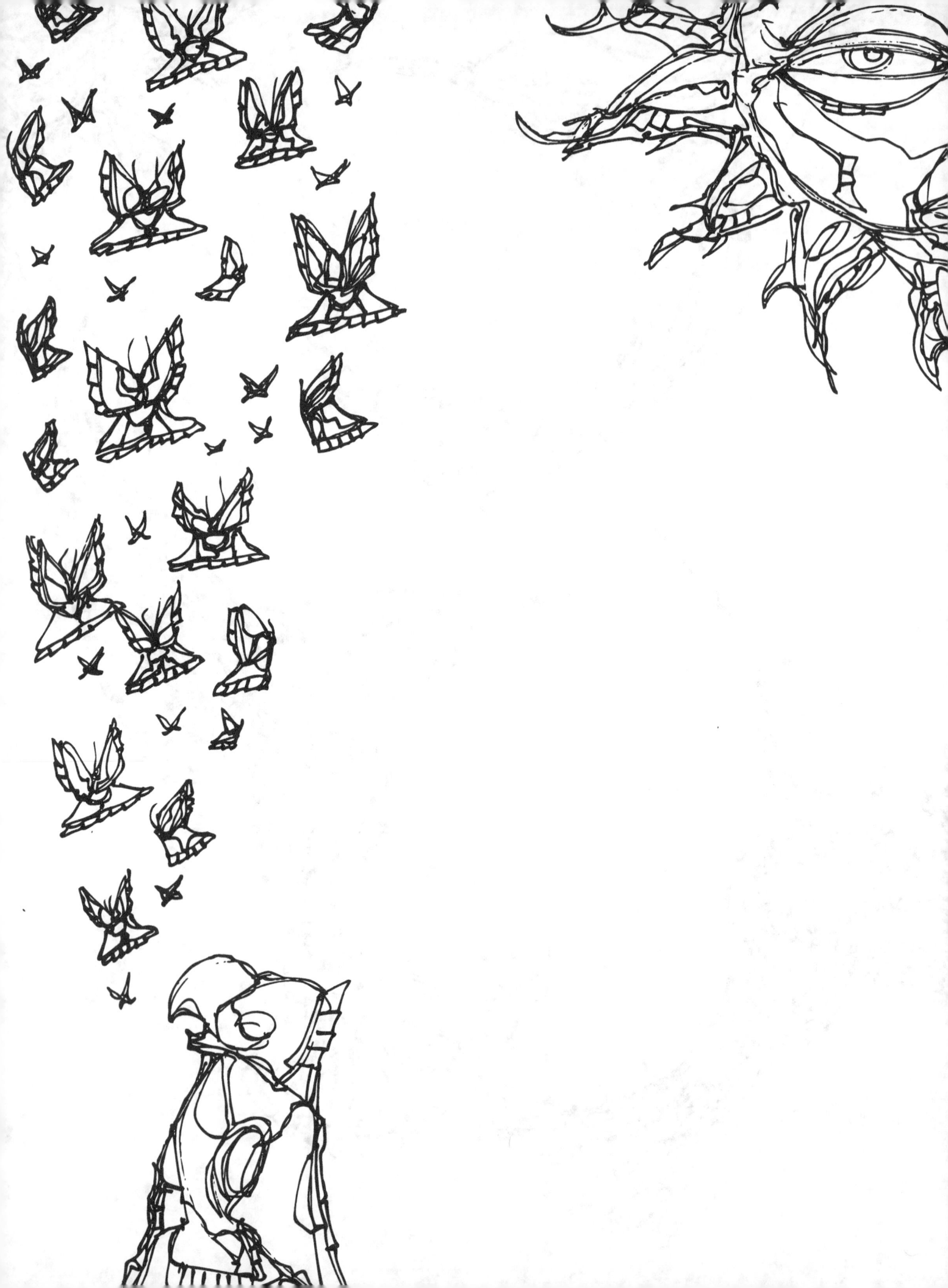

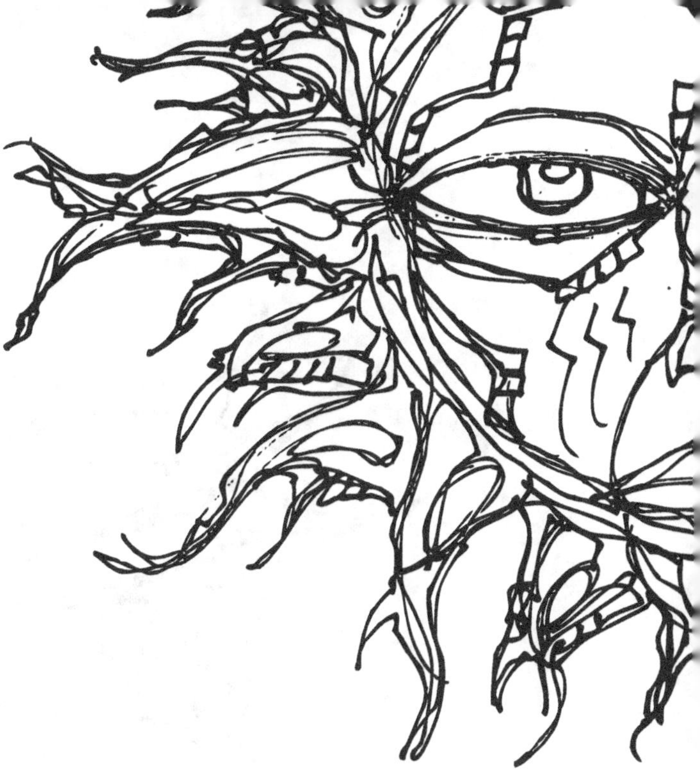

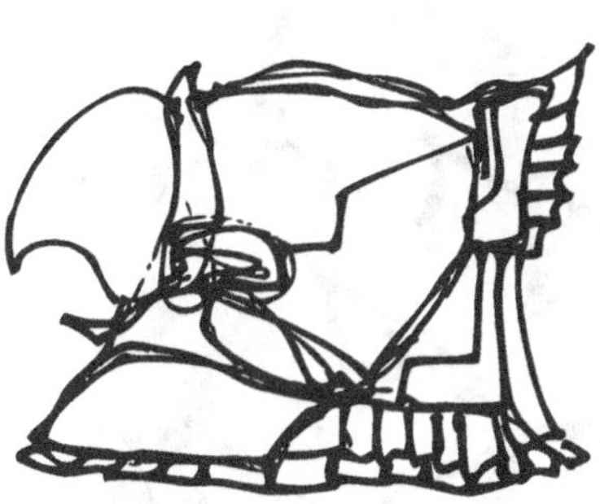

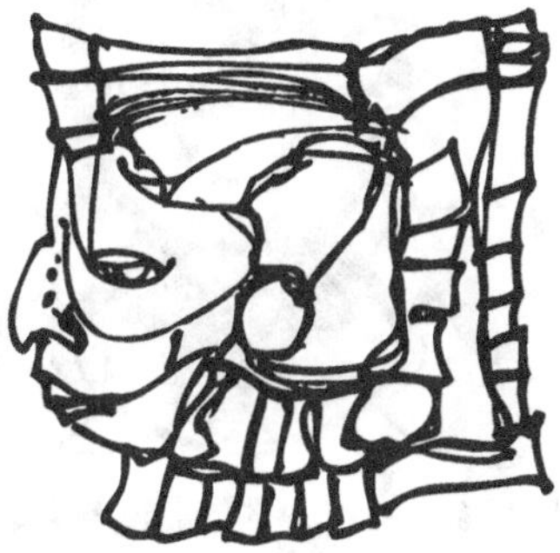

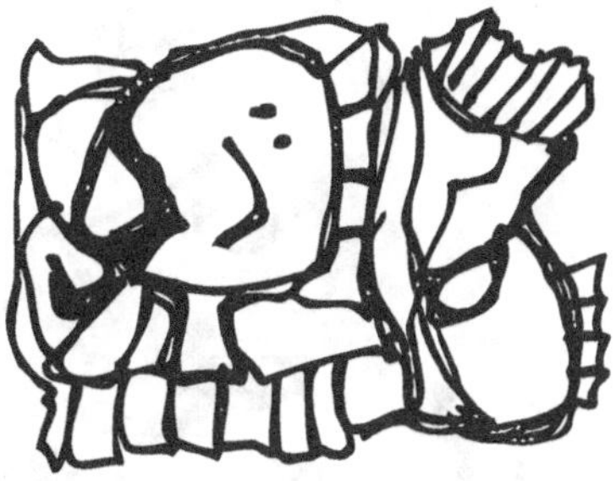

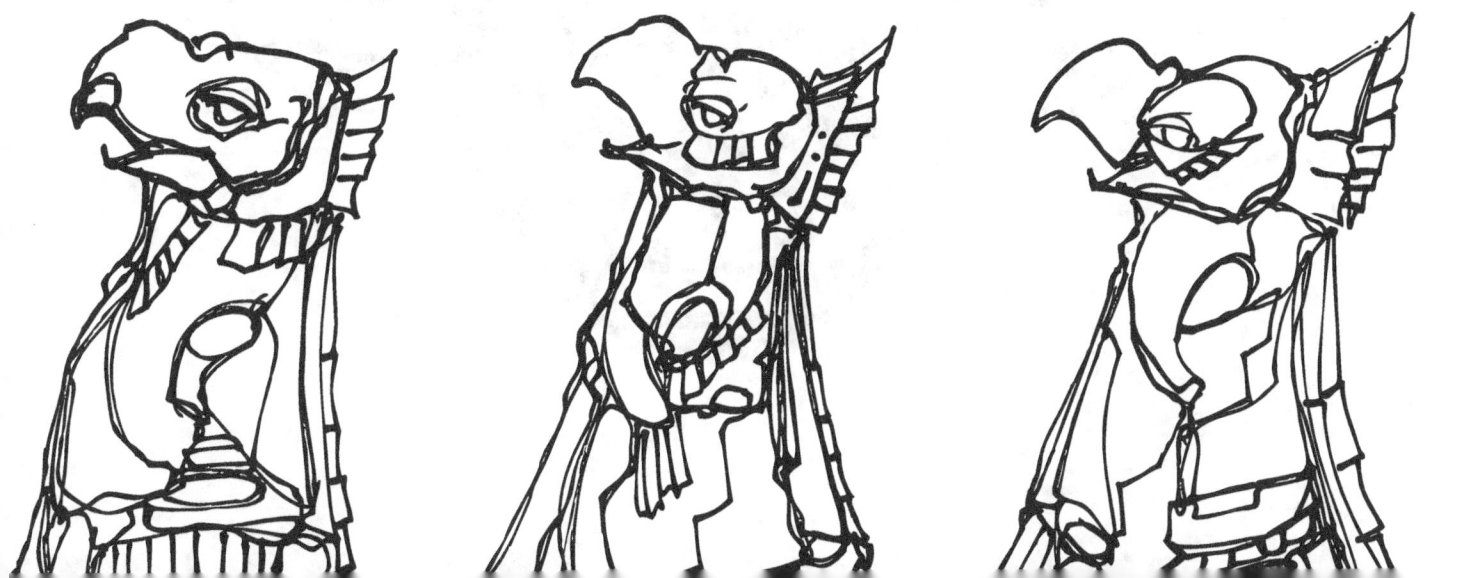

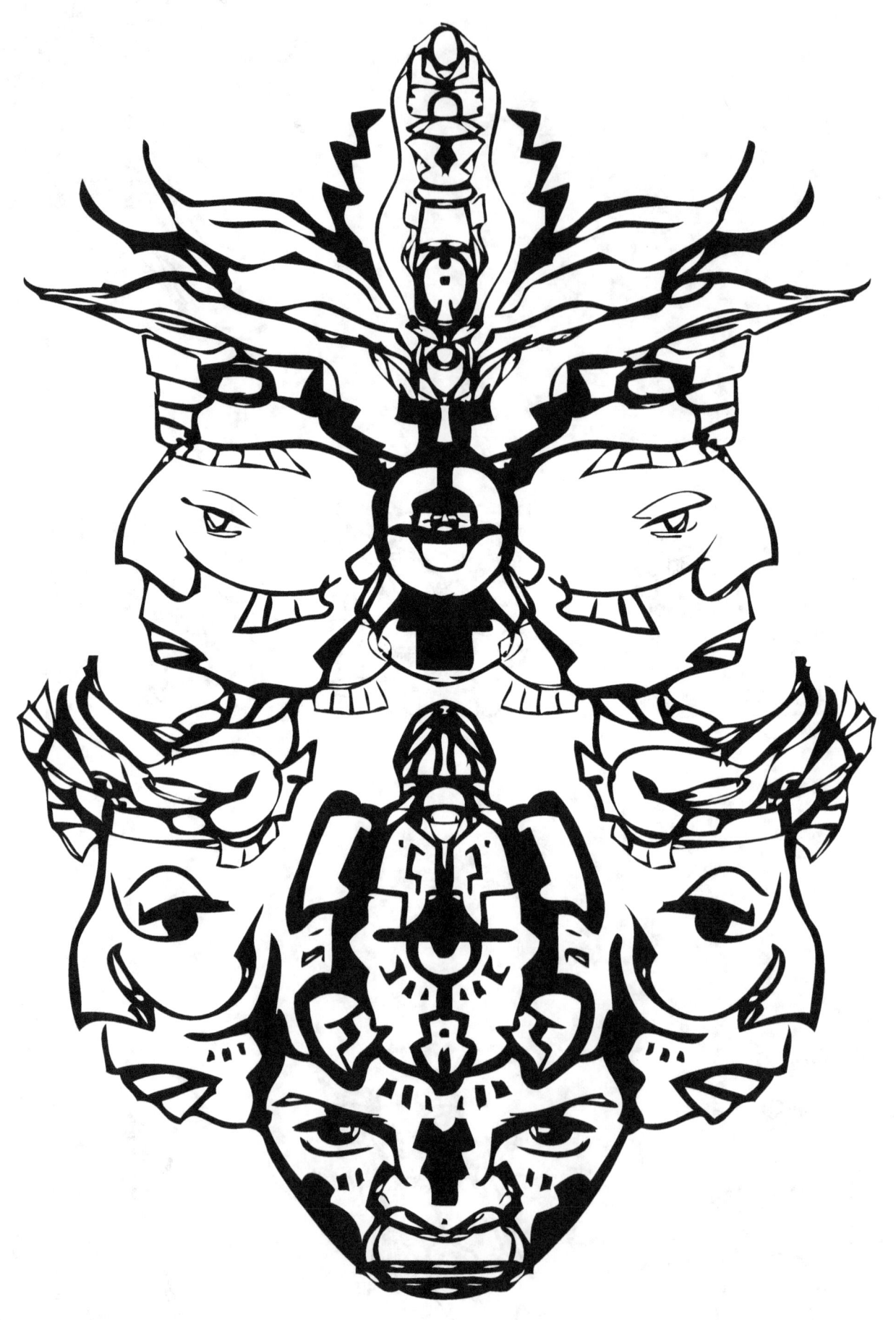

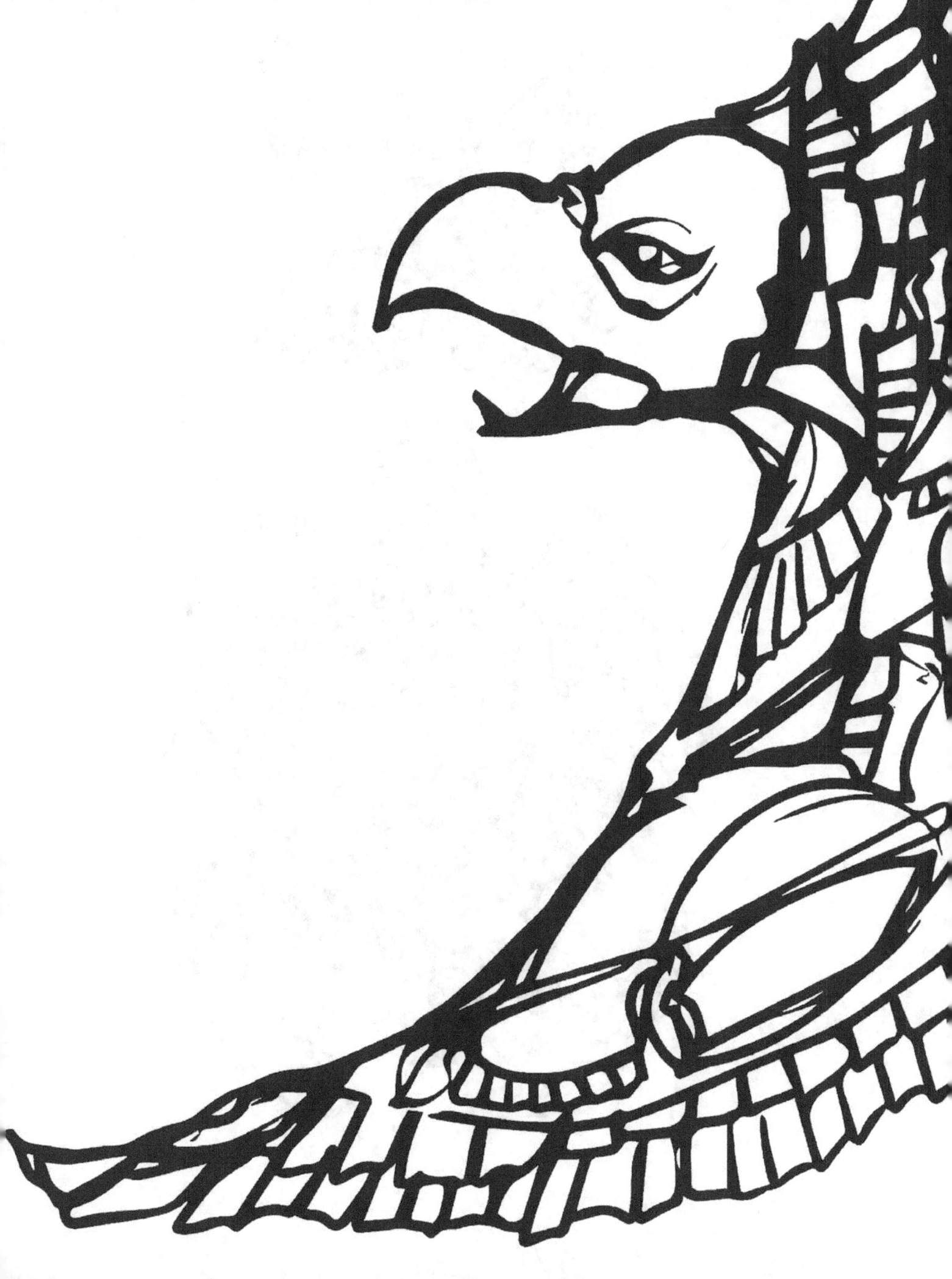

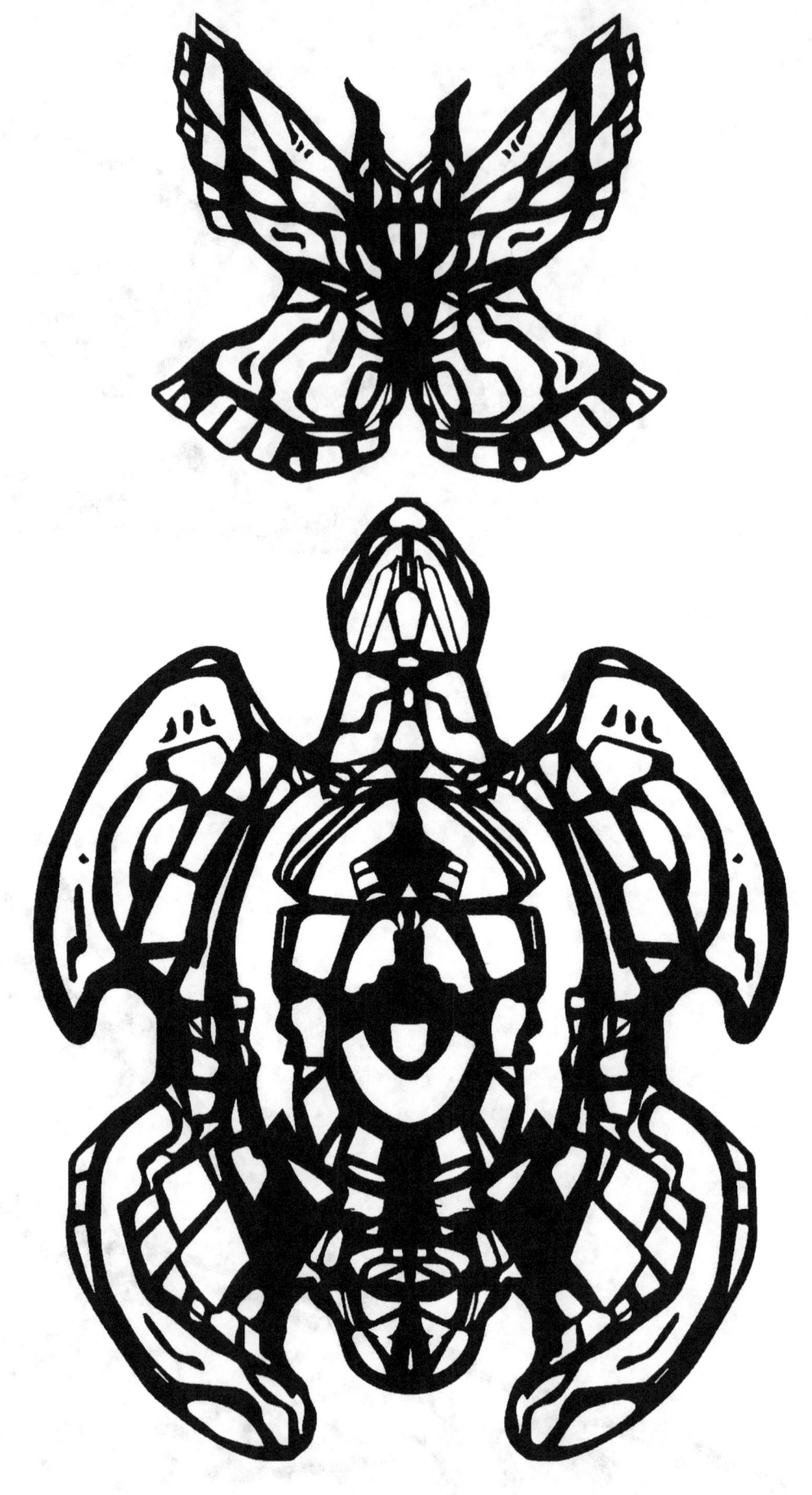

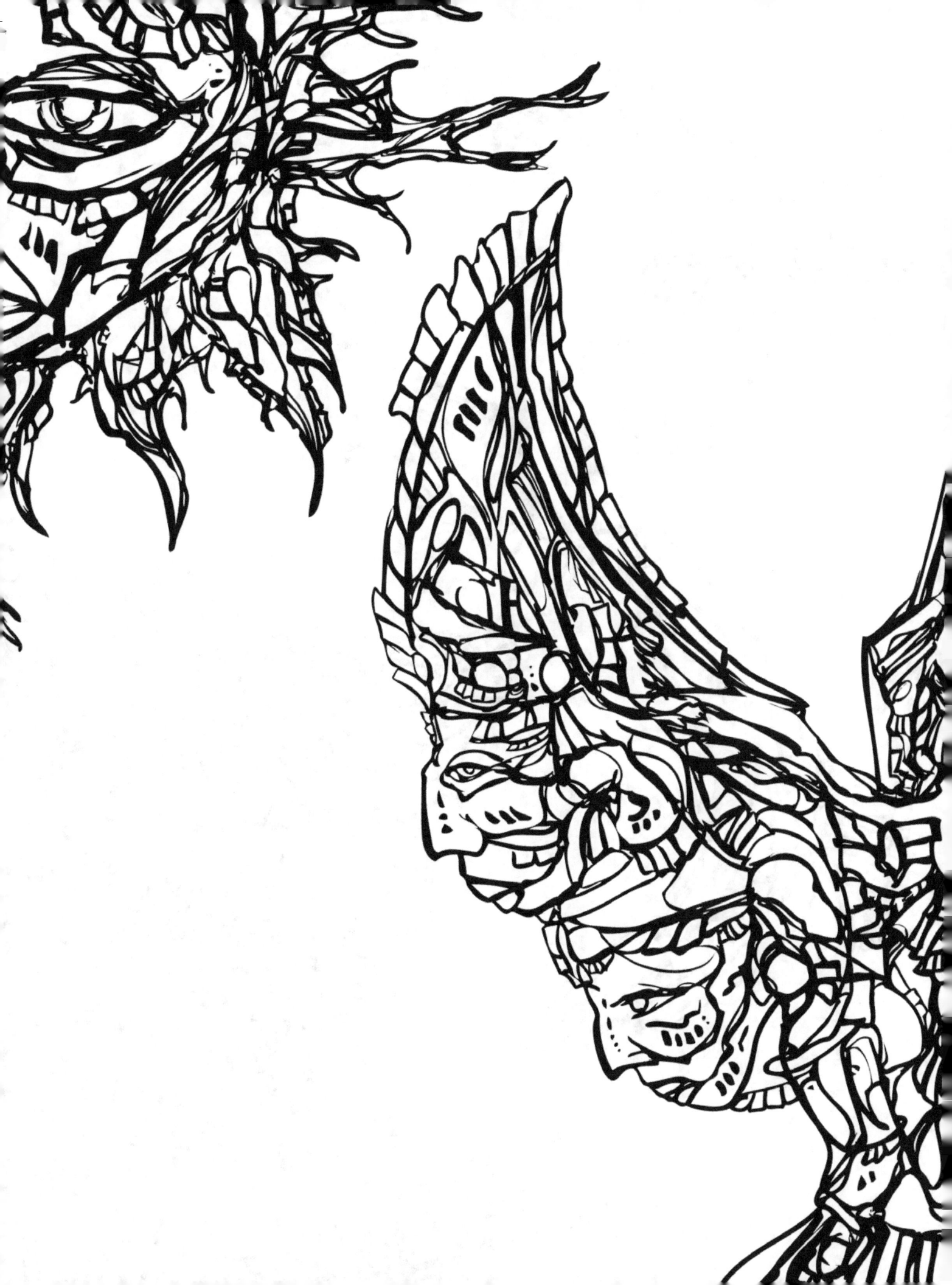

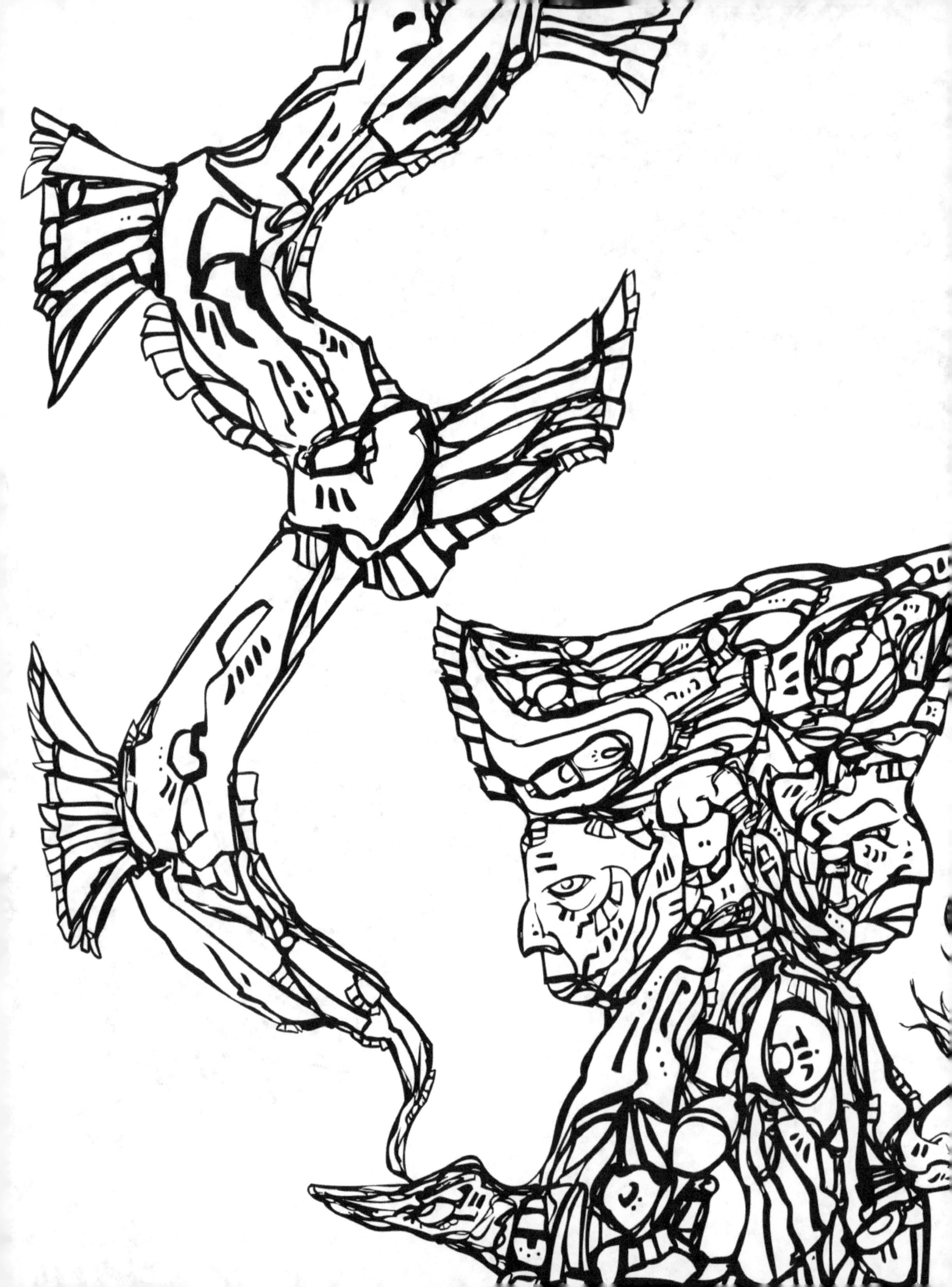

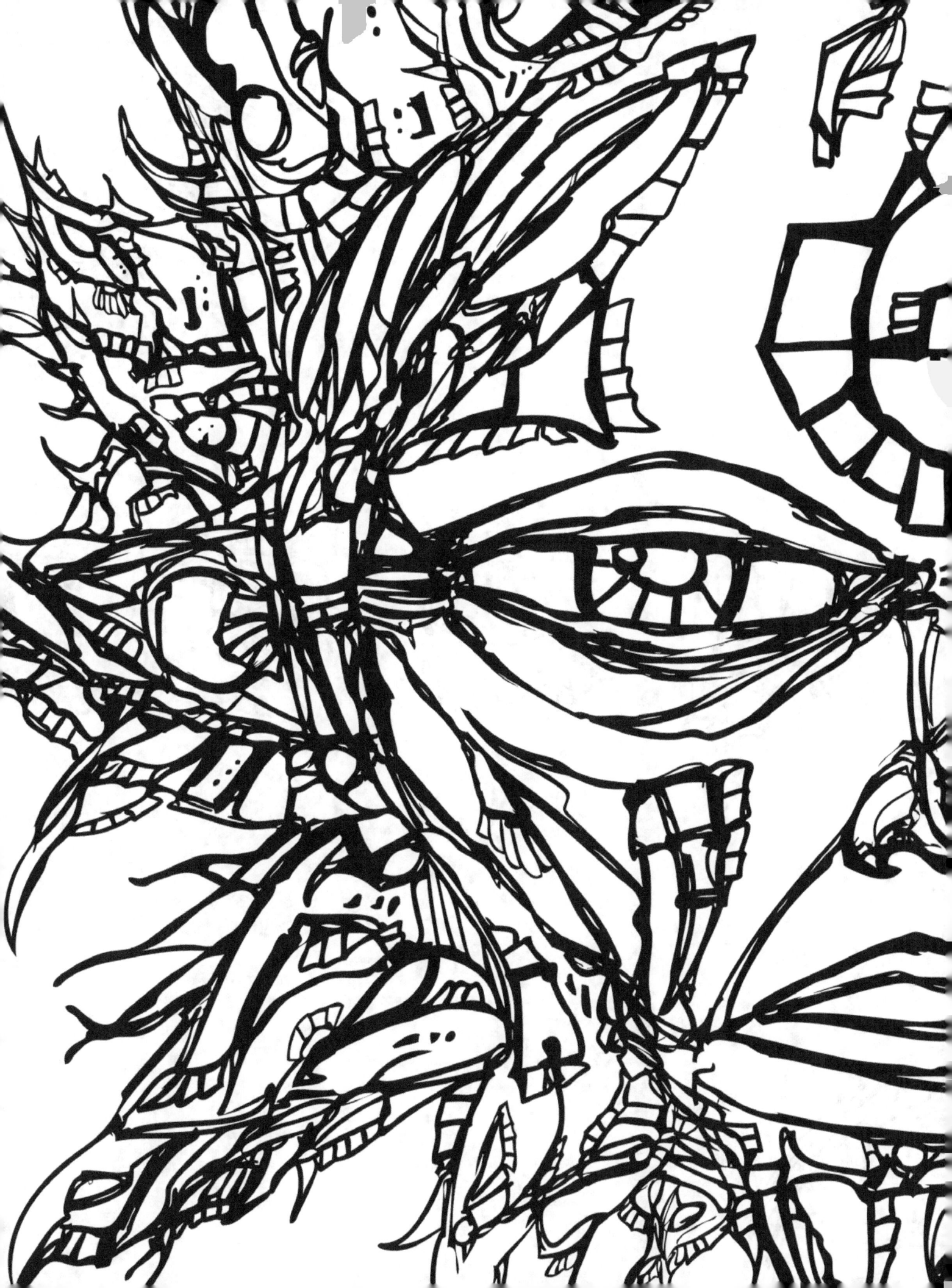

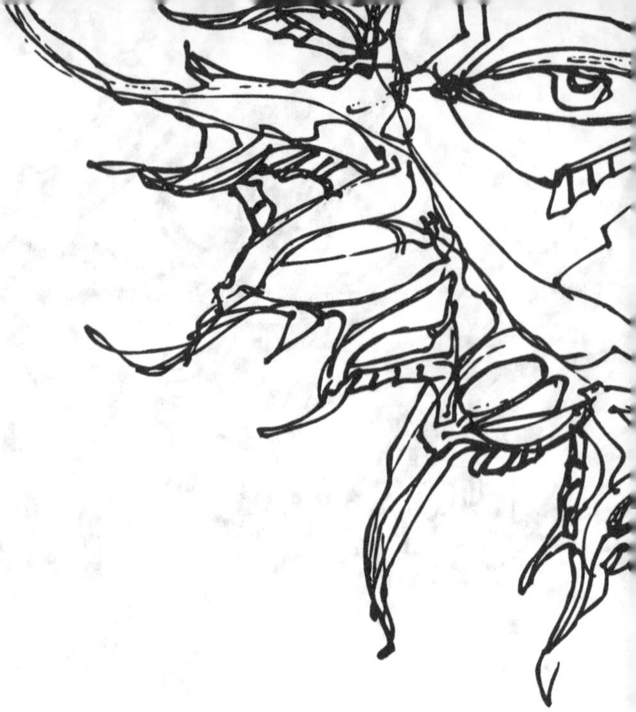

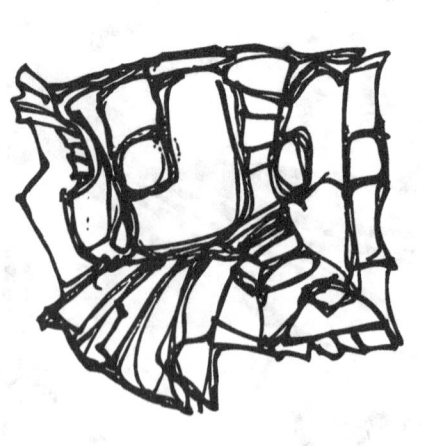
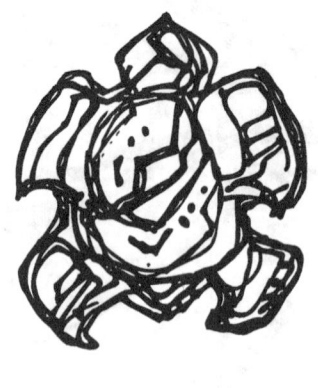
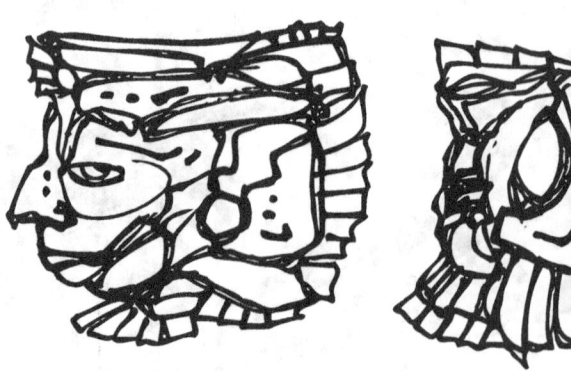
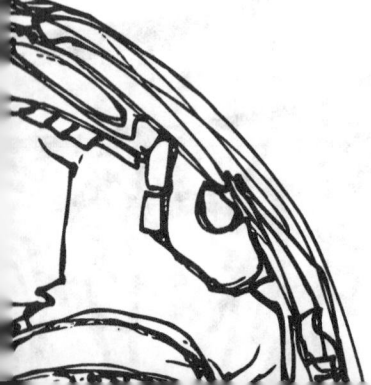